Metric Conversion Table

Inches (in.)	1/64	1/32	1/25	1/16	1/8	1/4	3/8	2/5	1/2	5/8	3/4	7/8	1	2	3	4	5	6	7	8	9	10	11	12	36	39.4
Feet (ft.)																								1	3	3¼†
Yards (yd.)																									1	1 1/10†
Millimeters* (mm)	0.40	0.79	1	1.59	3.18	6.35	9.53	10	12.7	15.9	19.1	22.2	25.4	50.8	76.2	101.6	127	152	178	203	229	254	279	305	914	1,000
Centimeters* (cm)							0.95	1	1.27	1.59	1.91	2.22	2.54	5.08	7.62	10.16	12.7	15.2	17.8	20.3	22.9	25.4	27.9	30.5	91.4	100
Meters* (m)																								.30	.91	1.00

To find the metric equivalent of quantities not in this table, add together the appropriate entries. For example, to convert 2⅝ inches to centimeters, add the figure given for the centimeter equivalent of 2 inches, 5.08, and the equivalent of ⅝ inch, 1.59, to obtain 6.67 centimeters.

*Metric values are rounded off.
†Approximate fractions.

Conversion Factors

To change:	Into:	Multiply by:
Inches	Millimeters	25.4
Inches	Centimeters	2.54
Feet	Meters	0.305
Yards	Meters	0.914
Miles	Kilometers	1.609
Square inches	Square centimeters	6.45
Square feet	Square meters	0.093
Square yards	Square meters	0.836
Cubic inches	Cubic centimeters	16.4
Cubic feet	Cubic meters	0.0283
Cubic yards	Cubic meters	0.765
Pints (U.S.)	Liters	0.473 (Imp. 0.568)
Quarts (U.S.)	Liters	0.946 (Imp. 1.136)
Gallons (U.S.)	Liters	3.785 (Imp. 4.546)
Ounces	Grams	28.4
Pounds	Kilograms	0.454
Tons	Metric tons	0.907

To change:	Into:	Multiply by:
Millimeters	Inches	0.039
Centimeters	Inches	0.394
Meters	Feet	3.28
Meters	Yards	1.09
Kilometers	Miles	0.621
Square centimeters	Square inches	0.155
Square meters	Square feet	10.8
Square meters	Square yards	1.2
Cubic centimeters	Cubic inches	0.061
Cubic meters	Cubic feet	35.3
Cubic meters	Cubic yards	1.31
Liters	Pints (U.S.)	2.114 (Imp. 1.76)
Liters	Quarts (U.S.)	1.057 (Imp. 0.88)
Liters	Gallons (U.S.)	0.264 (Imp. 0.22)
Grams	Ounces	0.035
Kilograms	Pounds	2.2
Metric tons	Tons	1.1

THE FAMILY Handyman ®

Decks, Patios, and Porches

THE FAMILY Handyman ®

Decks, Patios, and Porches

Plans, Projects, and Instructions for Expanding Your Outdoor Living Space

Reader's Digest

THE READER'S DIGEST ASSOCIATION, INC.

Pleasantville, New York / Montreal

A READER'S DIGEST BOOK

Produced by Roundtable Press, Inc.
Directors: Susan E. Meyer, Marsha Melnick
Executive Editor: Amy T. Jonak
Project Editor: David R. Hall
Editor: David A. Kirchner
Assistant Editor: Abigail A. Anderson
Design: Sisco & Evans, New York
Editorial Production: Steven Rosen

For The Family Handyman
Editor in Chief: Gary Havens
Special Projects Editor: Ken Collier
TFH Books Editor: Spike Carlsen

Library of Congress Cataloging in Publication Data
The family handyman decks, patios, and porches : plans, projects, and
   instructions for expanding your outdoor living space.
        p. cm.
    Includes index.
    ISBN 0-89577-852-1
    1. Decks (Architecture, Domestic)—Design and construction—
Amateurs' manuals. 2. Patios—Design and construction—Amateurs'
manuals. 3. Porches—Design and construction—Amateurs' manuals.
    I. Reader's Digest Association. II. Family handyman.
TH4970.F36   1996
643'.7—dc20   95-44744

A Note from the Editor

For most of our lives, we have equated being kept indoors with sickness, punishment, or some duty we'd rather ignore. When we were little, chicken pox and mumps meant solitary—indoor—confinement. When we stepped across the boundary of good behavior, we were sent to our rooms. Sunday school was never held in the sunshine, always in some moldy church basement.

Grade school, it seemed, was an endless wait for recess, the end of the school day, or summer vacation. In high school, we skipped class to hang out on warm spring afternoons. (Some even got away with it; I didn't.)

And now, as adults, we exchange our freedom for a paycheck, earned in oily machine shops, hermetically sealed office buildings, dark warehouses.

Is it any wonder, then, that as homeowners we dream of lounging in the open air—on a deck, patio, or porch of our own?

Is it any wonder that, once some researcher discovered how to pressure-treat wood with preservatives, the sales of that distinctive green-colored wood became the bread and butter of every home center and lumberyard in America?

And is it any wonder that *The Family Handyman Magazine* has published scores of projects aimed at increasing the homeowner's ability to relax in the clean, quiet outdoors—and that they are among our most popular ones?

No, there's no mystery to it. These projects answer virtually every homeowner's dreams. That's why you'll find the best of those projects right here. Like all TFH projects, we've built them before printing them—we've made the mistakes so you don't have to.

So now that you've paid your indoor dues, it's your turn to dream, to build, and to enjoy—outdoors.

Gary Havens

Editor in Chief, *The Family Handyman*

Decks, Patios, and Porches

Introduction

Homeowners often go to great lengths to improve the insides of their homes, focusing attention and loving care on every nook and cranny. But many of us forget about the largest area of all, the outside. All of the projects in *The Family Handyman Decks, Patios, and Porches* encourage you to think of your yard as one great outdoor room that you can readily, and affordably, improve to better enjoy your time at home.

Many of these projects are attractive permanent additions to your home that call for advanced carpentry skills, but even if your do-it-yourself experience is limited, you'll be able to tackle some of the ideas you'll find here. If a particular project is complex, we break it down into manageable, fully illustrated, step-by-step sequences and concentrate on explaining the finer details.

Working safely is critical to all of these projects. Some require concrete demolition (to remove a stoop), heavy lifting, or overhead work and the use of ladders (to frame and build a roof). They all involve the use of power tools and equipment. Always wear an appropriate dust mask and eye and ear protection, and always work only with sharp, well-maintained tools in accordance with their manufacturer's instructions. If you encounter stages that require skills you don't have or that you feel uncomfortable doing yourself, don't hesitate to engage a qualified professional for that part of the job.

Finally, be sure to involve your local building inspector at the planning stages, not only to ensure that your design is acceptable but also to solicit that person's expertise on how best to proceed.

Remember, the time and energy you devote to any of these projects will pay off in two ways: you'll own a new deck, patio, or porch to enjoy for years to come, and you'll have the pride and satisfaction that comes with completing a job well done.

Decks

Deck Builder's Companion

There's really nothing complicated about building a first-rate deck right in your own backyard. A deck's exposed structure lets you see how all the pieces fit together, from the bottom up.

The deck shown at right is the model for these step-by-step guidelines for building your deck. We'll explain fundamentals and suggest alternate techniques at every stage. By the end of this chapter, you'll be able to design, plan, and build your own deck like a pro.

Suggestions for Getting Started

Good planning and design will yield more deck for your time and money. Here are some startup tips that apply to all decks.

▷ With a pad and pencil, draw a sketch of the deck you'd like to add to your home. Don't worry about making an artistic rendering; just jot down as many of your ideas as you can.

▷ Now fill out the details in your sketch. Look at other decks in your neighborhood for examples of features you like. Check remodeling magazines and look through this and other books for ideas; clip or copy pictures of decks that appeal to you.

▷ Walk around your proposed deck site with a tape measure and figure out the deck's rough length, width, height, and elevation. Make a note of any unusual features and potential problems, like a slope or nearby trees. Then use these measurements to prepare a more detailed sketch.

▷ Take this design to your local building inspector's office. The staff there will be able to review your plan, help you determine the right sizes and types of wood for beams and joists, check the design and specifications of your railings, and tell you if you'll need a building permit. Discuss your plans with a building inspector in as much detail as you can provide. The people in that office are there to help you build the best and safest deck possible.

▷ If it won't compromise the aesthetics of your deck's design, consider using beams one lumber size larger than required. The extra strength will not only make your deck feel more solid but will also add to its safety and longevity. To determine the correct beam size for your deck, consider the weight or load the beam must carry, the beam's span (the distance between its support posts), and the kind of wood you're using.

For most decks, two pressure-treated 2x10's nailed together and supported with posts every 6 feet will be strong enough. But ask your building inspector to confirm that this size and span will work for your deck design.

▷ Review your plan and draw up a materials list, perhaps using as a guideline the items listed on page 14. Without counting every board and bolt, calculate as nearly as possible what you'll need. Then add 10 percent to your lumber and materials estimates to compensate for flaws in materials and for possible construction errors.

▷ Take your materials list and plan to a lumberyard for an estimate of the cost of materials. Lumberyard personnel can be very helpful, but respect their time. Avoid shopping on Saturdays, when they're likely to be busiest. When you explain your plan, be receptive to any new ideas and construction techniques they may suggest.

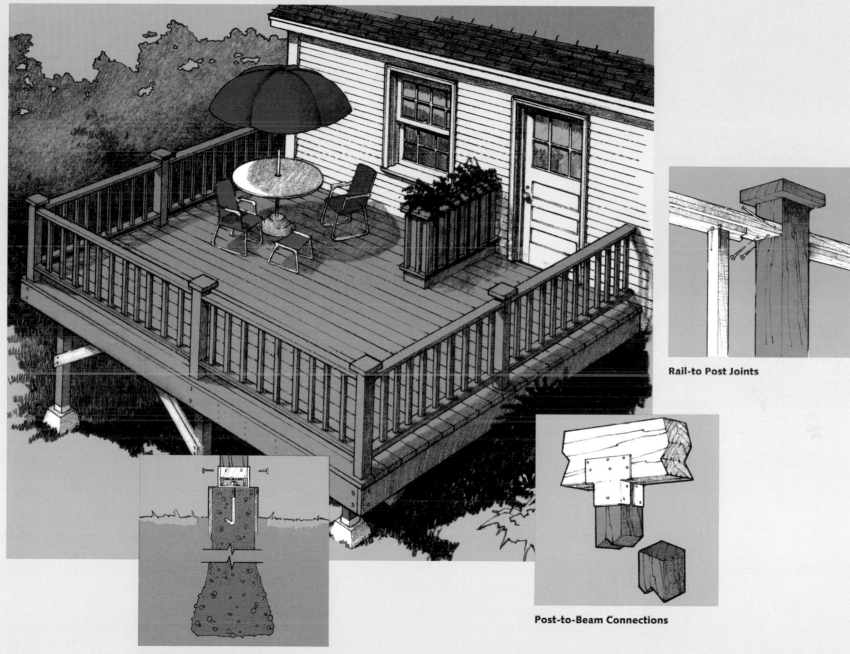

Rail-to Post Joints

Post-to-Beam Connections

Footings and Post Anchors

Inspect the actual lumber you'll be buying. Avoid wood that appears wet, because as it dries it will shrink and may even twist and warp. Choose material that's dry, straight, and free of splits, cracks, and excessive knots. Also compare different kinds of deck boards and railing materials. Quality varies, so if what you see doesn't meet your expectations, check what another lumberyard has.

Now price all the materials and come up with a total. Ask about any extra fees for delivery. Also, ask about quantity discounts.

Once the lumber has been delivered, it's time to lay out your post and footing locations. This can be tricky, especially on sloped sites. If you're unsure of your ability to measure accurately, consult this and similar books on deck building or ask someone who understands layout principles to check your work.

Finally, give yourself plenty of time to build the deck. If the job takes longer to complete than you estimated, remember that the quality you achieve will be worth the investment.

Suggested Lumber and Materials Checklist

Lumber	Quantity
Ledgers	
Posts	
Beams	
Joists	
Decking	

Stairs
  stringers
  treads
  risers	

Railings
  posts
  balusters
  rails	

Other Materials	Quantity
Silicone caulk	
Paint	
Stain	
Sealer	
Concrete: see Estimating Concrete, page 16	

Hardware	Quantity
Flashing	
Joist hangers	
Nails, screws, bolts, etc.: see Construction Plans	

Deck Building Basics

Before starting to work, take a few minutes to make sure you are completely familiar with the basic techniques required to complete your project.

Cutting a Post to Length

Square, accurate cuts can be troublesome when a post or beam is too thick to saw through in one pass (Photos 1–3). The trick is to draw a pencil line completely around the post with a framing square. Then, before you cut, check the angles of the saw blade with your square, to be sure it is exactly 90 degrees. Finish the cut with a handsaw if the power saw won't reach the center.

Notching a Post for a Beam

Beams must be supported by blocks bolted to the sides of the post ends or set in notches, rather than simply bolted to the side of the post. That way the notch, rather than the shanks of the bolts, carries the weight of the deck.

Notching a post is much easier if you do it in advance of installation, when you can lay the post across sawhorses and use the beam as a pattern to measure the width and depth of the cut (Photos 4–7). Pay particular attention to knots, which don't chip out easily. Cut extra kerfs in them.

Note that in this photo sequence the sample post shown is a 6x6. If you cut a 1-1/2 inch notch into a 4x4 post, you will critically weaken the post. Avoid doing this where strength is important.

Photo 1. Draw a line around the post, using a framing square for accuracy. The ends of all the lines must meet exactly.

Photo 2. Cut one side with a power saw, rotate the post 1/4 turn, and continue the cut in the same kerf. Cut all four sides.

Photo 3. Complete the cut with a handsaw if necessary, since a power saw blade won't reach the center of a 6x6 post.

Photo 4. Outline the size of the beam on the post, then set your saw blade's depth to the beam's thickness.

Photo 5. Begin sawing just inside one mark. Cut a series of kerfs 1/2 in. to 3/4 in. apart. Make many close cuts through hard knots.

Photo 6. Break out the chips with a chisel or hammer. Chisel the remaining rough areas flat; they don't have to be perfectly smooth.

Photo 7. Check the fit. Widen the notch with more saw cuts if needed. Try for a close fit; you can always widen the notch if necessary.

Build a Solid Foundation

Decks are versatile. You can put them just about anywhere you like and build them almost any way you want. But wherever you locate one and however you design it, start with a good foundation to ensure that your deck will hold up under years of hard use. In fact, in most parts of the country the local building inspector will insist that you do this, and may even impose a few other structural requirements. These guidelines are intended to help you build a deck that's both safe and solid.

Footings

Your deck's foundation has to shoulder the weight of the deck itself and the weight of all the furniture and people on it, so make sure it's strong. For most deck designs, 4x4 posts spaced every 6 feet, resting on a good base, will provide enough support.

Examine the options in the details at the right. Notice in the "Good Foundation" diagram that the bottom section of concrete, called the footing, must rest on undisturbed soil, because soil that has been loosened compresses too easily. The bottom of the footing must also be flat, to transfer weight evenly, and it must be at least 6 inches below the frost line in your area (your local building inspector will be able to tell you how deep to dig). This precaution is necessary to keep the footings from sinking or lifting and throwing your deck askew. Sink foundation holes by using a posthole digger or, if you have a lot of holes to dig, renting an 8-inch power auger. Widen and flatten the bottoms of the holes to make a good support base.

Post Anchors

Before you mix and pour the concrete for the footings, decide how you'll want to attach the 4x4 posts to them (refer to the alternatives on the facing page). Generally, steel connectors, available from lumber-yards and home centers, are the strongest. Like the 4x4 posts themselves, they should be set at least 6 inches above the ground, because continual contact with ground moisture will otherwise prematurely rust the connectors and rot the posts. Raising the footings above grade level also lets connectors and posts dry quickly. Always use rot-resistant (pressure treated) wood for support posts, or else the heartwood of redwood or cedar. With pressure-treated wood, look for a rating of at least .40 (ground contact); .60, or foundation grade, is better.

Although it's accepted practice in the construction industry to set supports directly into the ground like fence posts, doing so will accelerate rot (see Detail 2 on the facing page) and make it more difficult to replace rotted members.

Notice the two weaknesses of the footing option shown in Detail 1 (opposite) that make this type of footing unacceptable. First, although the metal connector is a good one, it won't last long, because water can easily pool around it and cause it to rust. Always build footings at least 6 inches aboveground so water is able to run off. Second, the footing is wider at the top than it is at the bottom, which will let frost catch its sides and heave it upward. Shape the holes for your footings so that they're wider at the bottom than the top.

Estimating Concrete

Should you mix your own concrete, or order it ready-mixed and have it delivered? To find out, estimate the volume of concrete you'll need and compare prices. Concrete is normally sold by the cubic foot or cubic yard. Typically, 4 footings 8 inches in diameter poured to a depth of 2 feet will require 3 cubic feet of concrete; for the same footings poured to a depth of 4 feet allow 6 cubic feet of concrete; for half the number of footings allow half (1-1/2) cubic feet of concrete, and so on.

Most concrete "flatwork" such as for sidewalks and patios is 3-1/2 to 4 inches thick. One cubic foot of concrete will create a surface 1 foot by 3 feet, or 3 square feet, and 4 inches deep. One cubic yard will create 81 square feet of a 4-inch thick slab.

Hand-Mixed Concrete. For an area smaller than 20 square feet, consider mixing bags of concrete in a wheelbarrow, tray, or drum, then dumping it in place.

For areas between 20 and 50 square feet, it makes sense to rent an electric- or gas-powered drum mixer. These machines mix 2 to 5 cubic feet at a time and dump the concrete where you want it.

Haul-It-Yourself Trailer Loads. Hand-mixing concrete for projects larger than 50 square feet is time consuming and you might not be able to pour the concrete quickly enough for all of it to harden together.

Many rental yards and ready-mix plants offer trailer loads of haul-it-yourself premixed concrete. A trailer can carry up to one yard of concrete. Transporting a 500-pound trailer and its 3,500 pounds of concrete from the supplier to your house requires a trailer hitch and may be too taxing for a small car. There's also the danger that the mix will settle unevenly en route, which would create a weaker bond.

Ready-Mix Truckloads. For a project larger than 100 square feet—beyond the skills of most do-it-yourselfers for a first-time project—order a ready-mix truck and plan to have plenty of help on hand when it arrives. Also make arrangements for dealing with heavy trucks once they arrive on your property.

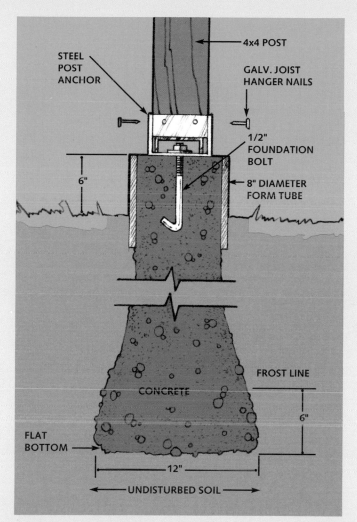

STEEL POST ANCHOR

4x4 POST

GALV. JOIST HANGER NAILS

1/2" FOUNDATION BOLT

8" DIAMETER FORM TUBE

6"

FROST LINE

CONCRETE

6"

FLAT BOTTOM

12"

UNDISTURBED SOIL

A Good Foundation

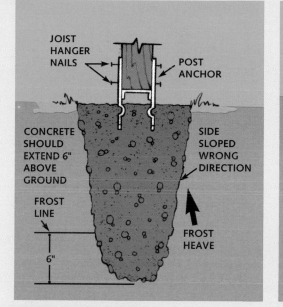

JOIST HANGER NAILS

POST ANCHOR

CONCRETE SHOULD EXTEND 6" ABOVE GROUND

SIDE SLOPED WRONG DIRECTION

FROST LINE

6"

FROST HEAVE

Detail 1. A Bad Foundation

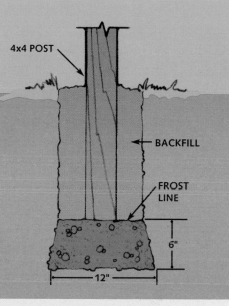

4x4 POST

BACKFILL

FROST LINE

6"

12"

Detail 2. An Acceptable Alternative

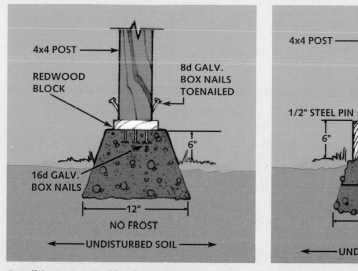

4x4 POST

REDWOOD BLOCK

8d GALV. BOX NAILS TOENAILED

6"

16d GALV. BOX NAILS

12"

NO FROST

UNDISTURBED SOIL

Detail 3. An Acceptable Alternative

4x4 POST

1/2" PREDRILLED HOLE

1/2" STEEL PIN

FORM 3/4" x 8" WOOD SQUARE

6"

6"

8"

12"

NO FROST

UNDISTURBED SOIL

Detail 4. An Acceptable Alternative

Install Beams and Posts

Think of your deck as a platform set across two or more strong horizontal beams. One of the beams, shown in the Framing Detail (below left), is made from two 2x10's spiked together with 16d galvanized nails atop 4x4 support posts. The other beam or ledger is bolted to the rim joist (or wall studs) of the house, (see the Ledger Support Detail, below, right).

Hanging the Ledger

▶ Install the ledger first, especially if you have a door that opens onto the deck. If that's the case, make the finished deck 1/2 inch lower than the door's sill, so you won't have an awkward step to negotiate as you pass through the door. After determining the appropriate ledger height, remove the house siding to about 1 inch above that point, so that you can screw the ledger tightly against the sheathing and house frame. You may have to use a power saw to cut the siding (see the Framing Detail, below left). Then slip aluminum flashing up under the siding, against the sheathing. Later if you have a concrete house foundation, you'll cut a groove into the concrete to anchor the flashing, as shown in the Ledger Support Detail (below right), then bend the flashing over the top of the ledger to keep water from collecting against the house and causing rot.

▶ Tack the 2x8 ledger in place temporarily with 16d nails. Level it and then attach it permanently with lag bolts, spacing the bolts about every 16 inches. Use 3/8-inch lag bolts that are 3-1/2 inches long so that they completely penetrate the ledger. Predrill the screw holes 1/4 inch. Use longer bolts if needed.

▶ Bolt the ledger to a concrete foundation if necessary (see the Ledger Support Detail). In that case, predrill holes for lag shields made of lead or for expansion bolts, using a hammer drill and a special carbide bit. For additional support, lag-bolt 2x4 blocks under both ends of the ledger.

▶ Finally, cut a 1/4-inch deep groove in the concrete to anchor the flashing. Snap a chalk line, then cut the groove with a circular saw, using a carborundum (not carbide) blade. Now fold the flashing down into the groove. Whenever you cut or drill in concrete, wear safety goggles, a dust mask, and gloves.

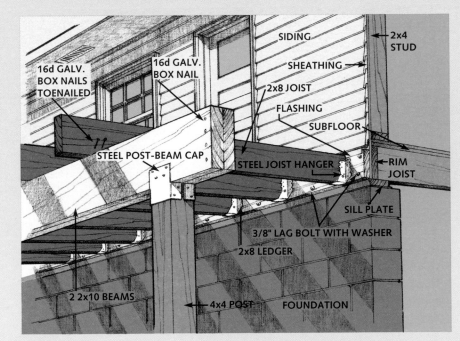

Framing Detail

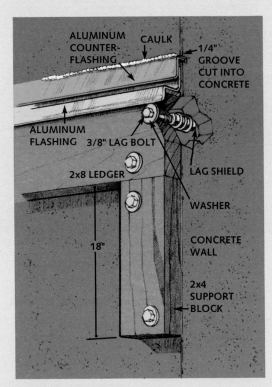

Ledger Support Detail

Erecting the Posts and Beams

When the ledger is in place, you can use it as a height reference for the opposite beam. Cut the 4x4 support posts to length, fasten them to their concrete footings, plumb them with a level, then temporarily brace them with boards. Now set the beam on top and nail it in place.

Posts, beams, ledgers, and joists support the deck's weight. Make them strong, and be sure to fasten them securely. The steel post-beam cap shown in Detail 1 below is the strongest type of post-to-beam construction. Because it spreads the weight of the deck over the entire end of the support post, it stresses the post's wood fibers the least.

The connection alternatives shown in Details 2 and 3 are adequate, but they will weaken sooner than the connection in Detail 1. Note that they use two different kinds of galvanized bolts—smooth-head carriage bolts and hexagonal-head machine bolts. Carriage bolts look neater for joints in which the bolt heads will be visible, but they can slip when you tighten them, making it hard to draw them up firmly. Machine bolts don't look as clean as carriage bolts, but they are easier to install, since you can steady their heads with a wrench.

Except for very low decks, it's a good idea to reinforce posts and beams with diagonal braces, to keep the deck from swaying (see the illustration on page 13). Check your posts with a level to make sure they're perfectly vertical, then bolt on 2x4 or 2x6 braces between the posts and beams at a 45-degree angle. The triangular support created by the beams, posts, and braces will keep the structure rigid.

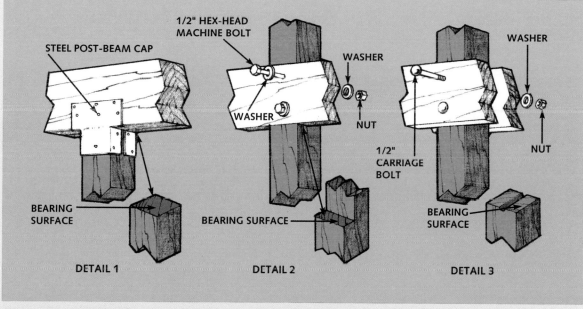

Post-to-Beam Connections

Assemble Joists and Decking

After you've completed the main structural work, add the deck's platform.

▶ Nail on the joists. Where they butt directly into a beam or ledger, fasten them with metal joist hangers. Where they rest on top of the beam, toenail them with three 16d galvanized box nails (as shown in the Framing Detail on page 18). Be sure to buy the proper size joist hangers, and nail through all holes with galvanized joist-hanger nails, also known as galvanized truss nails.

▶ Cap the ends of the joists with a band joist (see the Guardrail Detail below and the Decking Layout on the next page). Nail it securely to each joist with galvanized 16d nails, using three nails per 2x6, four per 2x8, five per 2x10, and so on.

As with beam size, proper joist size depends on the weight you'll be supporting, the distance the joists have to span, and the wood they're made of. Again, always confirm with your building inspector that the joist size you plan to use will work with your deck design. As a rule of thumb, if you space your joists 16 inches on center (o.c., from the center of one joist to the center of the next), a 2x6 will span 8 feet, a 2x8 will cover 10 feet, and a 2x10 will span 12 feet. Your deck will feel more solid, however, if you limit your joist spans to 8 feet. Remember, you can always add another beam to support the joists mid-span if you need to.

Guardrail Posts

▶ Before you add the deck boards, attach the posts for the guardrail. Strength and safety are the priorities here, so attach the posts to the joists with 1/2-inch carriage bolts as in the detail at left. One big advantage of using bolts instead of nails is that you can easily retighten them if they loosen. If your 4x4 deck support posts extend above the beams (as shown in Details 2 and 3 of the Post-to-Beam Connections options on page 19), you can use them for rail posts.

Don't skimp with your guardrail design.
▶ Bolt your guardrail posts securely to the joists and beams.
▶ Use 2x6's or 4x4's for posts.
▶ Build in enough posts. Plan on placing at least one every 6 feet.

The ultimate test of your posts is whether they feel solidly connected to the framework when you push on them. Even if your guardrail design meets the local building requirements, don't hesitate to beef it up if it just doesn't feel right or if you don't have confidence in its structural integrity.

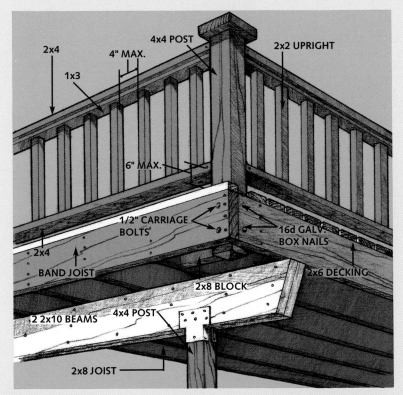

Guardrail Detail

Decking

Once the guardrail posts are in place, lay the decking. Nail the first board alongside—but not touching—the house, driving two 16d galvanized nails at each joist. Angle the nails toward the center of the board, as shown in the diagram below.

Here are some other tips for laying decking:

Space the boards with a 16d nail. If your deck is in a densely wooded area, consider spacing the deck boards the width of a carpenter's pencil, to let sticks, nuts, and other debris fall through.

Nail the ends of bowed boards first, forcing the bow against the previous row. Then drive a wide wooden shim between the rows to space the bowed board properly.

Make clean joints by cutting boards off perfectly square and butting them together over the center of a joist.

Near board ends, predrill nail holes to avoid having boards split.

Let the boards extend beyond the edges of the deck. Then trim them flush with the end joists after all the decking is down.

Decking Layout

Install the Railing

Design the railing so it's at least 36 inches high and a 4-inch ball (in most localities) can't pass between any uprights. The top rail needs to be the strongest—2x4 stock at a minimum. It's also the most visible railing component, so be sure to select your best-looking material for it.

Rails that pass over the tops of the posts are strongest and easiest to attach. Simply nail them into the posts with 16d galvanized box nails. Other designs, like the one shown in the Rail-to-Post Joint diagram below, require careful nailing to ensure strength.

Predrill all nail and screw holes.

Use 10d galvanized casing nails on the edges of the 2x4s and 2-inch No. 10 galvanized screws beneath.

If your design calls for a bottom rail, make sure it's of at least 2x4 stock. All other material should be 2x2 stock or stronger.

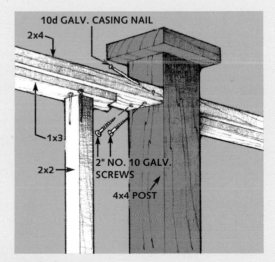

Rail-to-Post Joint

Showcase Deck

No one will blame you if you steal a little time to relax on this showcase deck.

Spacious and strong, this design incorporates decorative yet practical details that will make it the talk of the neighborhood.

The deck's colorful tile is a striking feature, which also supplies the fireproofing required for the floor underneath a barbecue. Planters also do double duty by acting as safety barriers at the deck's edges. Slim steel intermediate guardrails offer an optimal view of the backyard. And the 6-foot screen wall is a privacy fence, windbreak, and sunscreen all in one.

Ceramic tile, built-in planters, horizontal pipe rails, and a decorative privacy screen distinguish this deck from the ordinary.

Deck Design Plan

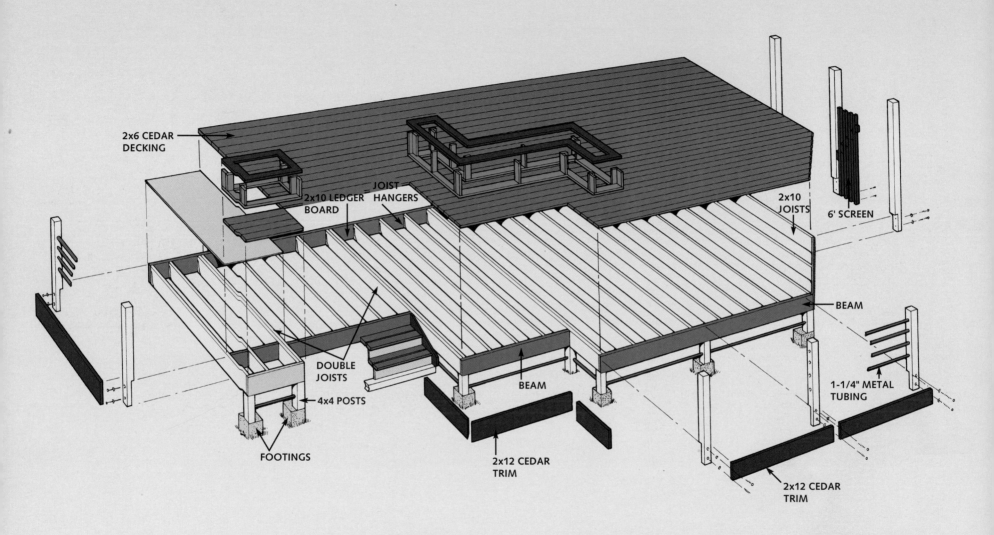

2x6 CEDAR DECKING

2x10 LEDGER BOARD

JOIST HANGERS

DOUBLE JOISTS

4x4 POSTS

FOOTINGS

2x12 CEDAR TRIM

BEAM

2x10 JOISTS

6' SCREEN

BEAM

1-1/4" METAL TUBING

2x12 CEDAR TRIM

Plan Your Deck

As attractive as it is, this deck is almost certainly too complicated for the first-time deck builder. If you've had experience working from straightforward deck plans, however, you should be able to assemble the basic framework, using the drawings and tips given here. Rely on your previous experience to build the actual deck. For a brief review of deck-building basics, see "Deck Builder's Companion" (pages 12–21).

Time Considerations

A deck this big will naturally take a long time to build. Allow up to two weeks to build the basic deck plus a full weekend each to add the railings, planters, tile, benches, and screen wall. If you're working alone, plan to give this project most of your free time for an entire summer. You might want to consider recruiting friends or hiring a helper to speed the work.

Careful planning is critical to any successful deck project, and one this large is definitely no exception. Begin by sketching a design for a deck to fit your site, like the one shown in the Deck Framing Plan Diagram on page 27. The drawing does not need to be a work of art, but be sure to include the size and location of all support posts, the size and spacing of the joists and beams, and a schematic of the railing. Then ask your local building inspector to review your plan to confirm that it meets the building code's requirements.

Materials and Tools

Next, use your plan to draw up a materials list and estimate the cost of the deck. If you find that the total cost exceeds your budget, you can wait to build the planters, the benches, or the screen wall. They are all very easy to add later.

The deck shown in this project was built using cedar for all the visible deck parts, because it's rot resistant and more attractive than pressure-treated wood. However, for the framework we did use pressure-treated wood, since it is less expensive, stronger, and longer lasting than cedar.

You can build this deck with standard hand and power tools like a jigsaw, but having a power miter box will save you time cutting out the many pieces that make up the planters, screen wall, and benches.

Mark Your Layout

It is important that you position your posts accurately for this irregularly shaped deck, because they will sit directly under the corners.

Drawing the Layout

The best way to draw an accurate framing layout is to start with a right triangle (see the dotted lines on the Deck Framing Plan, page 27). The sides of a triangle with a right angle always have a length ratio of 3-4-5.

▶ Draw a base line (top) and mark an origin point (left end). Attach here a string that is exactly 12 ft. long.

▶ Measure out 9 ft. on the base line and attach a 15' string there.

▶ Pull the ends of the strings together until they are taut. The 12' string is now 90° to the base line. Mark its path.

Transfering the Layout to Your Work Site

▶ Lay out the post positions with string lines and stakes. Use the house as a base line.

▶ Measure and set a string line parallel to the house and exactly 12 feet away.

▶ Stretch another string at a right angle to the house at one end of the deck. Making an accurate 90-degree angle is easy if you construct a triangle with 9-, 12-, and 15-foot sides (see the Deck Framing Plan).

▶ If the ground under the deck slopes more than a foot, level your string lines. If you make sure to keep them level, your layout will be accurate.

Tools You Need

Hand Tools

Crosscut and hole saws

Hacksaw

Hammer

Handsaw

String lines and stakes, chalk line, tape measure

Posthole digger

Screwdrivers

Socket wrench and sockets

Staple gun

Power Tools

Jigsaw and circular saw

Drill

Optional

Power auger, miter box, tile cutter

Construct the Deck

Attaching Ledgers to Masonry

If your house has a masonry exterior, ask your building inspector for the best way to attach ledgers. It may be better to pour footings and set posts against the house, leaving the ledger or house-side beam free, than to attach ledgers to the masonry. See further information on installing ledgers on page 18.

Dig the Footings

▶ Dig holes for the concrete footings with a posthole digger or a rented 8-inch power auger (see the Footing Detail, below left). The correct depth will depend on the location of the frost line in your region.

▶ To keep water away from the posts, build forms from 1-inch thick boards that extend the tops of the footings at least 6 inches above ground level. Carefully align the forms before you pour the concrete.

▶ After filling the holes and forms with concrete, insert a 4-inch galvanized steel rod 2 inches into the wet concrete, centered in the area of each post's footprint. Later you'll set the posts over these "drift pins" to keep them stable. Anchoring posts with drift pins works fine for low decks, but for decks higher than 3 feet use special steel post anchors, available at lumberyards.

A 2x10 ledger board lag-screwed to the house supports the other side of the deck (see the Deck Design Plan, page 24). When you install the ledger, slip a strip flashing up under the siding after you've cut it away (see the Ledger Board Detail, left). The flashing overlaps the ledger to keep water from collecting near the house and causing rot.

Frame the Deck

Now you are ready to frame the deck, using the Deck Design Plan (page 24) as a guide.

▶ Cut the doubled joists to length; nail them together with 16d galvanized nails spaced every 16 inches along each edge; and hang them from the ledger using metal joist hangers (see the Ledger Board Detail, left).

▶ Cut the posts to length so the doubled joists they support are level.

▶ Nail the beams to the doubled joists. To allow for the steel tubing that will later run between the posts underneath the railing, bore out the posts with a 1-1/2 inch hole saw, then cut and insert the tubing.

▶ Toenail the beams and doubled joists to the posts with 16d galvanized nails.

▶ Nail the rest of the joists to the ledger and beams, using joist hangers.

▶ To stabilize the framing further, you can attach a row of 2x10 blocks between the joists with 16d galvanized nails (Photo 1).

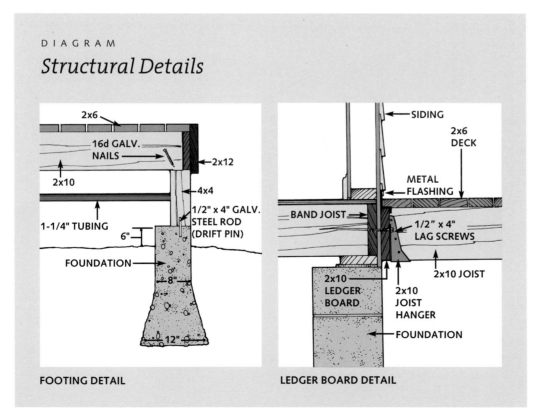

DIAGRAM
Structural Details

2x6
16d GALV. NAILS
2x10
1-1/4" TUBING
2x12
4x4
1/2" x 4" GALV. STEEL ROD (DRIFT PIN)
6"
FOUNDATION
8"
12"

FOOTING DETAIL

SIDING
2x6 DECK
METAL FLASHING
BAND JOIST
1/2" x 4" LAG SCREWS
2x10 JOIST
2x10 LEDGER BOARD
2x10 JOIST HANGER
FOUNDATION

LEDGER BOARD DETAIL

DIAGRAM

Deck Framing Plan

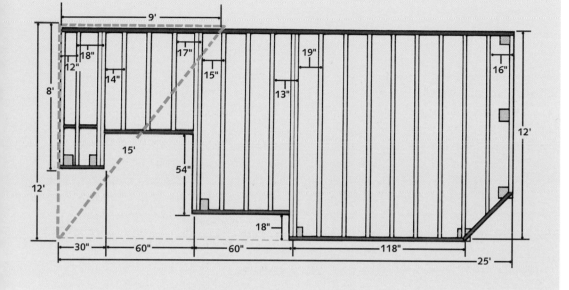

Lay the Decking

Before laying the 2x6 cedar deck boards, screw a sheet of 3/4-inch pressure-treated plywood to the joists to create a subfloor for the tile (Photo 2). Then butt the deck boards against the plywood's edges.

Because a deck board also serves as the top tread of the stairs, install that 2x6 first, laying it parallel to the house. To make it perfectly straight, snap a chalk line across all the joists and use it as a guide. In this project the deck boards are spaced 1/8 inch apart, using 16d nails to maintain even spacing. If you find that your last deck board will be less than 2 inches wide, use a 2x8 to finish up, to avoid having to lay a narrow strip. Fasten the 2x6 deck boards by driving two 3-inch galvanized deck screws into each joist. Screws will hold better than nails, and you won't risk denting the wood with errant hammer blows. Also, although it is slower, driving screws with a drill won't stress your wrist as much as hammering will.

Keep a drill with a 1/8-inch bit handy to predrill the deck boards near their ends so they won't split. As you work, let the ends of the boards run beyond the edges of the deck. Then, once all the decking is down, cut off the board ends all at once with a circular saw, using a guide board to keep the kerf straight as you cut.

Photo 1. Frame the deck with 2x10 joists and beams. A 2x10 ledger lag-screwed to the house supports one side, 4x4 posts the other. Blocking stiffens the joists.

Photo 2. Screw 3/4-in. pressure-treated plywood to the joists to make a subflooring for the tile. Secure the cedar 2x6's with 3-in. galvanized deck screws.

Railing Detail

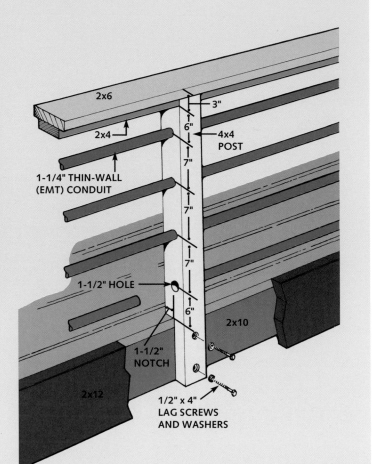

2x6

2x4

1-1/4" THIN-WALL
(EMT) CONDUIT

1-1/2" HOLE

1-1/2"
NOTCH

2x12

3"

6"

4x4
POST

7"

7"

7"

6"

2x10

1/2" x 4"
LAG SCREWS
AND WASHERS

Assemble the Railings

The steel railing tubes are actually sections of 1-1/4 inch thin-wall conduit, available in 10-foot lengths at home centers and electrical-supply stores.

▶ Use knot-free cedar 4x4's for the posts so that they remain strong even when large holes have to be bored in them (see the Railing Detail, left). Bore the holes with a 1-1/2 inch hole saw. When you have to drill completely through a post, first make a 1/4-inch guide hole all the way through, then bore the 1-1/2 inch hole partway through from each side.

▶ Where the pipe enters the posts at a 45-degree angle, cut a strip of scrap cedar at that angle and temporarily tack it to the 4x4. This strip allows you to start a 45-degree hole as usual, just as if it were entering the post at a right angle.

▶ To measure the tubing accurately, plumb the posts with a level and temporarily screw them in place. Predrill 1/2-inch holes through the cedar 4x4's, then make 3/8-inch pilot holes into the deck framing to accept the 1/2 x 4-inch lag screws.

▶ Now, with the posts in place, measure the tubing lengths, allowing each end to penetrate the post by about 3/4 inch. Cut the tubing to length with a hacksaw, then clean it with paint thinner to remove oil and grease, prime it with galvanized metal primer, and spray paint it to produce a smooth finish.

▶ Install the tubing (Photo 3). Cap the post tops with a 2x4 and a 2x6. Then nail the 2x12 cedar fascia boards between the posts.

Photo 3. Assemble the railing, using 1-1/4 in. thin-wall metal conduit for the intermediate rails. Bore holes in the posts with a 1-1/2 in. hole saw.

Construct the Planters

The simple design of these planters lets you adapt their size and shape easily to fit your deck without changing its basic plan.

▶ First, measure and cut the 2x4 frame members. Using a power miter box will save you time in cutting the nearly 50 short pieces that make up the planter frames (see the Planter Detail, below).

▶ Assemble the 2x4 framework for each side of the planter, using 16d galvanized nails. Nail each section to the deck, then secure the top 2x4, lapping it over adjacent sections to hold the top firmly (Photo 4).

▶ Line the planters with 1/2 inch pressure-treated plywood to contain the soil. Bore 3/4-inch holes in the planter bottoms, about 6 inches apart, to allow excess water to drain away. Use only galvanized nails and screws, to keep rust from forming.

▶ Sheath the outsides of the planters with 5/8-inch exterior-grade plywood. This type of grooved siding, called T1-11, is commonly available in 4x8 sheets at lumberyards and home centers. Tile or 1x2 cedar strips will cover the plywood edges at corners to prevent them from absorbing water.

Photo 4. Assemble the planter frames from pressure-treated 2x4's. Line the insides of the planters with 1/2-in. pressure-treated plywood.

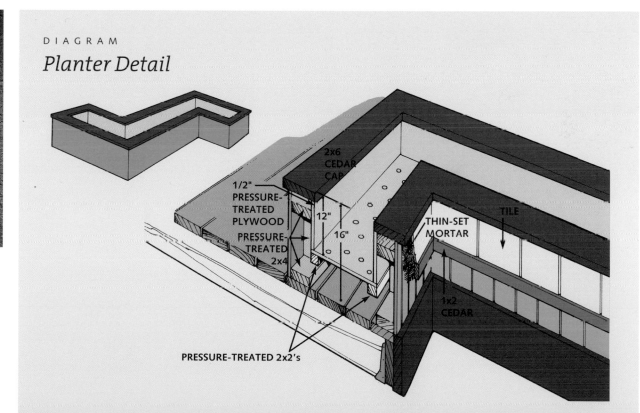

DIAGRAM

Planter Detail

2x6 CEDAR CAP

1/2" PRESSURE-TREATED PLYWOOD

PRESSURE-TREATED 2x4

12"

16"

THIN-SET MORTAR

TILE

1x2 CEDAR

PRESSURE-TREATED 2x2's

Set the Ceramic Tile

For this outdoor tile floor first lay a 1/2-in. layer of cement board. Durock and Wonderboard are two common brands. Glue and screw the cement board to the plywood subfloor. This will put the top surface of the tile about 1/4 inch above the surrounding deck, to help with water drainage (see the Tiling Detail, below).

The tile used here measured 8 inches square and was rated for use on floors. Make sure to buy floor-rated tile with a glaze that won't become slippery when wet.

▶ Where the tile fits around the corners of the planters, conceal the unglazed edges. As was done here, you can ask a tile specialist to cut a 45-degree angle on the corner tiles with a diamond-blade tile saw. Or you can simply use tiles that have colored edges, called bullnoses. Nailing 1x2 cedar strips to the corners of the planters and then tiling up to these cedar strips is another option.

▶ Dry-lay your tile on the cement board first, so you can check the spacing and cut the last row in advance. Rent a tile cutter or buy an inexpensive tile snapper. Your ceramic tile dealer can tell you the best way to cut the tile you choose.

▶ Set the tile in a thin-set mortar, spreading it with a 1/4-inch notched trowel (Photo 5). Most tile has built-in spacers, but use wood shims or plastic spacers if necessary. After the mortar hardens, spread the recommended type of grout over the tile surface and press it into the joints with a rubber trowel. Finally, clean the surface of the tile with a damp sponge and buff it down to a nice finish with a clean, dry cloth.

Protect Your Wood

Grout or mortar can leave ugly stains on the surrounding wood, so cover the wood with masking tape and drop cloths when it comes time to lay the tile.

DIAGRAM

Tiling Detail

GROUT LINES

8" TILE

3/4" x 3/4" CEDAR TRIM

2x6 CAP

1/2" PRESSURE-TREATED PLYWOOD

1/2" CEMENT BOARD

THIN-SET MORTAR

8" TILE

GROUT LINES

PRESSURE-TREATED 2x4

PRESSURE-TREATED 3/4" PLYWOOD

2x12 CEDAR

2x10

1x2 CEDAR

T1-11 5/8" EXTERIOR PLYWOOD

2x6 DECK

Photo 5. Lay the ceramic tile in thin-set mortar spread with a 1/4-in. notched trowel. Fill the gaps with grout, clean the surface with a damp cloth, then buff the finished tile with a dry cloth.

Assemble the Benches

Cut out the bench components, following the dimensions in the Bench Detail, below. Again, having a power miter box would be helpful. You'll also need a jigsaw to cut the curved side panels. Use clear (knot-free) cedar 2x2's for the seat slats. Round-over their edges to eliminate splinters. For this design the legs were attached to the deck with 10d galvanized nails, so the 1-1/4 inch steel tubing is purely decorative.

Since the benches are a permanent feature of the deck, it will be easier to build them in place. You can use either nails or screws for attachment hardware, but if you use screws always predrill the screw holes, to avoid splitting the cedar.

The most difficult cuts are the angled miters on the 2x2's along the fronts of the benches at the inside and outside corners. The easiest way to cut this angle is to tip each 2x2 at a 45-degree angle so that it rests in the miter box exactly as on the bench. Once all the pieces are cut, assemble the bench in the following steps.

▶ Nail the 2x6 trim board to the planter.

▶ Screw together the legs, frames, and 1-1/4 inch tubing. Then toenail the legs to the deck floor and the back trim board, making sure to plumb them with a level.

▶ Toenail the 2x4 corner supports to the trim boards. Support the front edges of the supports with temporary 2x4's.

▶ Nail the 2x2's and 1/2-inch spacers to the frames with 12d galvanized nails, starting at the back and working forward. At the corners, toenail them to the 2x4 supports, or screw them together from underneath.

▶ Nail on the end trim pieces (Photo 6).

Photo 6. Assemble the cedar bench, separating the 2x2's with 1/2-in. spacers. Cover the ends with a rounded 2x6 end cap mitered to the back 2x6 trim.

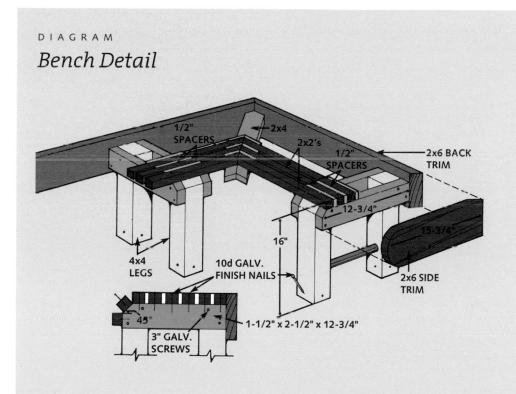

DIAGRAM

Bench Detail

Build the Screen Wall

The screen wall in this design serves as a deck-level privacy fence. It effectively blocks the area that you don't want to see—or be seen from—while leaving the rest of your view wide open.

Since the screen will be attached permanently, it can block out wind or sun only when they are coming from the correct direction. To block the wind more effectively you can hang large fabric panels over the back side. Vinyl-coated polyester mesh like that often used for lawn chairs and beach umbrellas is available at fabric stores.

▶ Assemble the screen by screwing cedar 2x2's to the deck framing and top rail (see the Screen Wall Details, right). Short 2x2 spacers keep the long 2x2's running straight and true and add a decorative pattern at the same time (Photo 7). Assemble the screen with 2-1/2 inch galvanized screws or 12d galvanized nails.

▶ To make the wind-screen panels, simply stretch polyester mesh across a frame made from 1x2 cedar. Fasten the edge with 5/16-inch staples (see the Screen Wall Details and Photo 8). If the deck will be exposed to strong winds, reinforce the frame by substituting 2x2's for the 1x2's or adding horizontal crosspieces.

Design on Paper

To design and duplicate your screen wall pattern, measure the space between posts and sketch the pattern on a sheet of graph paper. Once you've designed it, lay out all the 2x2's and spacer blocks to make sure the design fits. You'll probably need to shave some of the spacers slightly or make the last spacer a bit wider to fit the opening perfectly.

BUILD THE SCREEN WALL

Photo 7. Construct the screen wall by extending the railing posts 6 ft. above the deck. Screw 7-ft. cedar 2x2's to the deck frame, rail cap, and spacer blocks.

Photo 8. Staple polyester mesh onto 1x2 cedar frames to make wind screens. Hang them using hooks and eyes.

Screen Wall Details

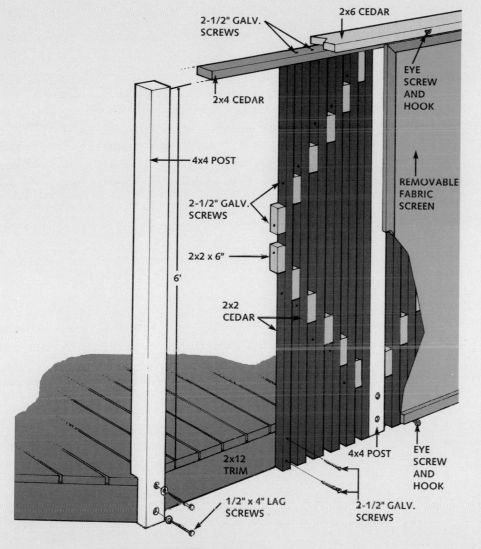

2-1/2" GALV.
SCREWS

2x6 CEDAR

2x4 CEDAR

EYE
SCREW
AND
HOOK

4x4 POST

2-1/2" GALV.
SCREWS

REMOVABLE
FABRIC
SCREEN

2x2 x 6"

6'

2x2
CEDAR

2x12
TRIM

4x4 POST

EYE
SCREW
AND
HOOK

1/2" x 4" LAG
SCREWS

2-1/2" GALV.
SCREWS

SCREEN WALL DETAIL

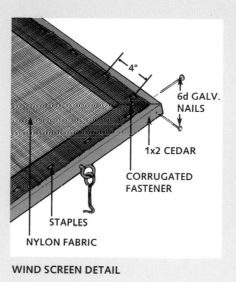

4"

6d GALV.
NAILS

1x2 CEDAR

CORRUGATED
FASTENER

STAPLES

NYLON FABRIC

WIND SCREEN DETAIL

Finishing Tip

Two coats of semitransparent exterior stain will be decorative while protecting the deck from moisture and sunlight.

Sunburst Deck

Even if there's not much room in your yard, you can get lots of enjoyment from this great small-scale project.

What this simple and compact sunburst deck lacks in size it more than makes up in elegance. What's more, even with its distinctive curves and decking inlays, the sunburst deck does not require super skills or a high level of experience.

Construction Plan

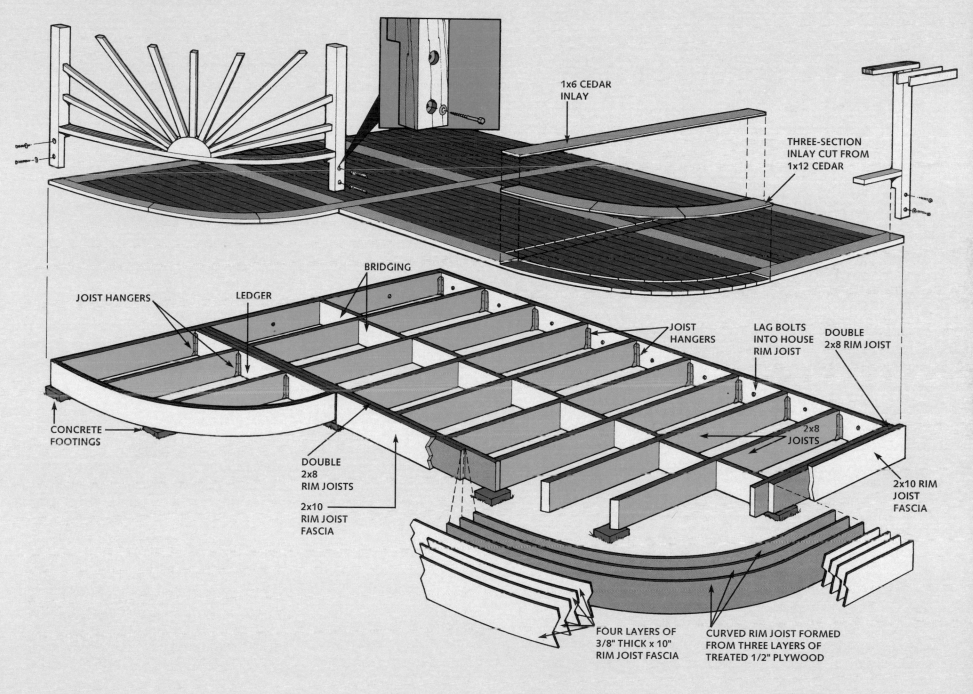

1x6 CEDAR INLAY

THREE-SECTION INLAY CUT FROM 1x12 CEDAR

BRIDGING

JOIST HANGERS

LEDGER

JOIST HANGERS

LAG BOLTS INTO HOUSE RIM JOIST

DOUBLE 2x8 RIM JOIST

CONCRETE FOOTINGS

DOUBLE 2x8 RIM JOISTS

2x10 RIM JOIST FASCIA

2x8 JOISTS

2x10 RIM JOIST FASCIA

FOUR LAYERS OF 3/8" THICK x 10" RIM JOIST FASCIA

CURVED RIM JOIST FORMED FROM THREE LAYERS OF TREATED 1/2" PLYWOOD

Plan Your Sunburst Deck

Tools You Need

Hand Tools

Clamps

Framing square

Hammer

Hand plane

4-ft. level

Socket wrenches

Straightedge

Posthole digger

Push broom

Steel trowel

Power Tools

Belt sander

Circular saw

Power drill/screwdriver

Router

Saber saw

Optional

Power auger (rented)

Surface planer (rented)

This deck's flexible size and shape will make it relatively easy to adapt to your own house and yard. You can make it longer or shorter, wider or narrower, without varying the basic design or construction procedures. If you decide to customize the plans, take special care to ensure that the lines of all the curved sections still flow together smoothly.

Before You Begin

The actual framing and construction of this deck are surprisingly straightforward, even for novice deck builders. The elegant finishing touches—the decking inlays, the curved bench and rails, and the sunburst balusters—will require patience and a bit of finesse, but no advanced skills or deck-building experience. The do-it-yourselfer with medium levels of skill and experience can expect to take about 150 hours to complete this deck.

You'll need only the more common power tools to build this deck: a circular saw, a saber saw, a heavy-duty power drill that doubles as a screwdriver, a heavy-duty router, and a belt sander. If you live where winters are severe and footings need to be deep, or if you have a lot of footing holes to dig, consider renting a power auger. The deck shown here uses pressure-treated lumber for all framing members and cedar for the decking, railings, and other visible parts.

Even though this design is structurally simple, obtain whatever permits your locality requires and have the deck inspected as needed. Don't hesitate to share your plans with your local building inspector, who can help you avoid design pitfalls before you start to build and may even be able to recommend some timesaving shortcuts.

Pouring the Footings

This deck design employs six concrete footings to support its perimeter rim joists (see the Construction Plan on page 35 and the Deck Layout on the facing page). In this plan the main support joists span only 8 feet. If your deck is wider than 10 feet, you should use joists wider than these 2x8's or else add footings to reduce the span by supporting the joists midway. Building-code requirements vary with the locality and the type of wood used, so always check with your local building inspector before firming up the details of your design.

▶ Dig the holes for the concrete footings and pour them so that they're broadest at their bases, to provide maximum support (see the Footing Detail on page 37; also see Build a Solid Foundation on pages 16–17 for more footing information). The footings must extend at least 6 inches below the frost line in your area (ask your building inspector for the acceptable depth).

▶ To determine the locations for the footings, draw your deck on paper, including the information shown in the Deck Layout. Show the joist lengths and thicknesses and the spacing between them as well as the radii of the curved portions. Now determine the footing locations, placing the footings so they extend no more than 1 inch beyond the faces of the rim joists. This step allows you to completely conceal the footings with wider fascia boards you will install later.

Because the rim joists rest directly on the footings, take special care to finish the footings at as close to the same height as possible, with level tops. Plan the footings so the final height of your finished deck falls about 1/2 inch below the bottom of the door's threshold (see the Ledger Board Detail on page 39).

▶ Build the footing forms from pieces of 2x8's nailed together to form an opening 8 inches square on the inside. Sink the forms partway into the ground around the footing holes. Find the proper height for the form nearest the sliding door by using a level and a long, straight board.

▶ Now align the tops of the other footing forms with the first one. Leave about 3/4 inch of space between the tops of the footings and the bottoms of the rim joists so you can level the deck with shims after you've completed the framing.

Deck Layout

Laying out your deck on paper allows you to judge approximately how much lumber you will need. You may want to add about 10 percent to your first estimate to allow for unusable pieces and cutting errors.

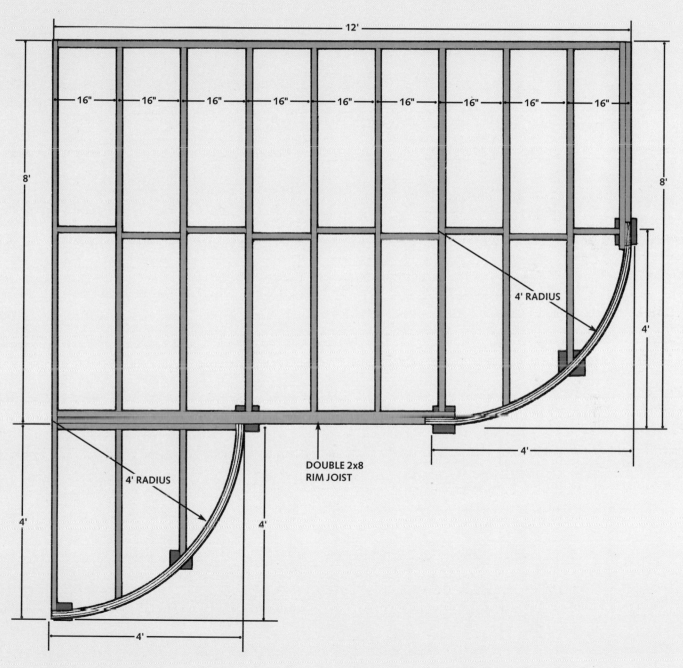

12'

16" 16" 16" 16" 16" 16" 16" 16" 16"

8' 8'

4' RADIUS

4'

4' RADIUS

4'

4'

DOUBLE 2x8 RIM JOIST

4'

4'

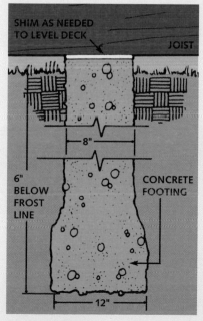

SHIM AS NEEDED TO LEVEL DECK

JOIST

8"

6" BELOW FROST LINE

CONCRETE FOOTING

12"

FOOTING DETAIL

Construct the Sunburst Deck

Frame the Deck

This deck is attached to the house with a ledger board (see the Ledger Board Detail on the facing page).

▶ Level the ledger board carefully, then mount it to the rim joist of the house by using 4-inch to 6-inch lag bolts that are long enough to secure it firmly. Apply a bead of caulk along the top of the joint where the ledger meets the house.

▶ If your house has horizontal beveled wood siding, you may have to cut some of it away so the ledger board can be mounted flat. If this is necessary, slide an L-shaped length of aluminum flashing up under the siding and over the top of the ledger to shed water. Then caulk the seams.

▶ Mark the positions of all the joist hangers on the ledger. Attach the hangers, using galvanized nails. (You may find that it is easier to attach the joist hangers before bolting the ledger to the house.)

▶ Place the 2x8 joists in position, supporting them at their opposite ends so they're level. Now measure and mark their exact lengths and cut them to size. Trim the joist ends that butt against curved rim joists, at the approximate angle of the curve.

▶ Nail the joists to the ledger-mounted joist hangers. Then nail 2x8 rim joists to the other ends of the joists and slip the joist hangers in place. Secure the hangers firmly to both the joists and the rim joists.

▶ Form the curved sections of the rim joists from three layers of 1/2-inch pressure-treated plywood. Bend each layer of plywood into shape individually, then screw it to the rim joist and the joist ends with galvanized screws (see the Curved Section Detail, opposite, and Photo 1, below).

▶ Add bridging to keep the joists from twisting or bowing out of position. Cut lengths of 2x8's to fit between the joists, then nail them in place. Offset these bridging pieces so that you can nail through the joists into the ends of the individual sections (Photo 2).

▶ Once all the framing is completed, level the deck by placing shims between the rim joists and the tops of the footings wherever they're needed (Photo 2). Use pressure-treated plywood for the shims. Apply a dab of construction adhesive to each shim to prevent it from sliding out of place.

FRAME THE DECK

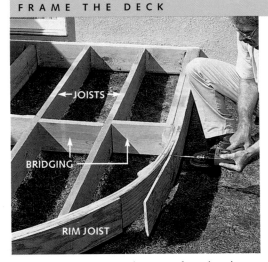

Photo 1. Construct curved rim joists from three layers of 1/2-in. treated plywood. Bend each layer separately, screwing it to the joists and rim joists.

Photo 2. Level the frame by prying with a 2x4, then shim with treated plywood between the rim joists and footings. Tack the shims with construction adhesive.

Framing Features

The ledger board is attached to the house rim joist. Then the deck joists are hung from the ledger. Finally, the curved sections of the rim joist are built up, adding one layer of plywood at a time.

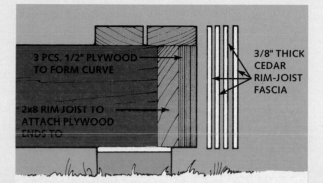

CURVED SECTION DETAIL

For tight curves and easier bending with 1/2-in. plywood sections like the ones used here, cut kerfs on the inside, closely spaced in tight curves and more loosely in wider-radius bends. Running the surface grain of the plywood lengthwise along the edge will also help make the bending easier.

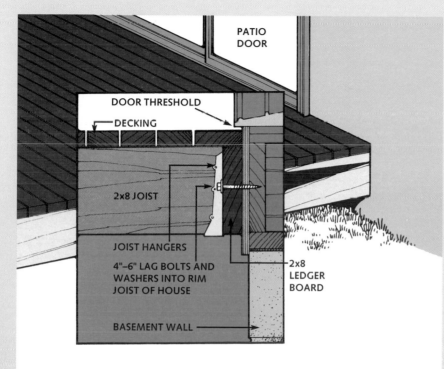

LEDGER BOARD DETAIL

Lay the Decking

With the framing finished and leveled, lay out the 2x4 cedar deck boards. Use 16d nails as spacers to maintain a 1/8-inch gap between boards.

▶ Attach the deck boards with two 2-1/2 inch galvanized decking screws at each joist. Set the screw heads slightly below the deck's surface. If you plan to rout recesses for decking inlays, lay them out now. Avoid driving screws in those areas until after you've cut the recesses.

▶ If you need to make a joint in a run of decking, cut the board ends perfectly square and position the joint over the center of a joist. Stagger the joints wherever possible, for the best appearance and greatest strength. Allow all the board ends to overhang the rim joists. When all the decking is down, cut these ends flush with the faces of the rim joists. Use a circular saw for straight edges and a saber saw for curves (Photo 3).

▶ For the straight inlays, cut recesses 1/4 inch wider than the boards, to maintain spacing on each side. The inlays of this deck are 1x6 cedar boards. Cut the outside edges with a circular saw and a straightedge. Set the blade depth at 3/4 inch (Photo 4). Then rout the recess with a 1/2-inch flat-bottom straight bit (Photo 5).

▶ For the curved inlays, allow side spacing as well. Contour the inside edge of each recess, using a curved router guide of plywood. Cut the inlay from three pieces of 1x12, mitering the ends to butt neatly.

▶ Secure the inlays in the recesses with galvanized decking screws. Let the inlay boards overhang the curved rim joist by 1/8 inch. Once all the inlay boards are down, cut them off with a router fitted with a straight trimming bit.

LAY THE DECKING

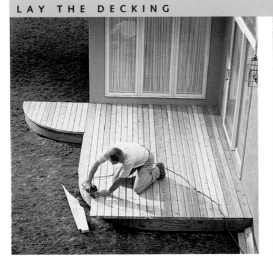

Photo 3. Trim the deck-board ends flush with the rim joists after laying all the decking. Cut straight edges with a circular saw, curved edges with a saber saw.

Photo 4. Cut edges for the straight recessed inlays with a circular saw and a straightedge guide. Set the blade 3/4 in. deep, the thickness of the 1x6's.

Photo 5. Rout out the recesses with a 1/2-in. straight-shank router bit. Form curved recesses using a guide cut from 1/2-in. plywood.

Build the Railings and Balusters

The vertical railing posts for this project are cedar 4x4's, notched to fit over the rim joists and decking (see the Railing Detail on the next page).

▶ Secure the posts to the rim joists with lag bolts. On curved rim joists, mount 2x8 backup pieces behind them. Check that your lag bolts are long enough to hold firmly.

▶ Make the horizontal railing members from standard nominal 4-inch beveled cedar siding, which is actually 3-1/2 inches wide, laminated together to form the curves (see the Railing Detail and Photo 6). Cut most of the siding lengthwise down the middle. These half-width pieces are used to form the lower rail and the center section of the top rail, which rests on the 4x4 posts. The full-width pieces make up the outer sections of the top rail and extend over the post sides.

Photo 6. Build up curved rails by gluing and screwing together 4-in. beveled cedar siding. Use half-width siding for the inner-rail sections, alternating the bevels.

▶ Form the top rail curves by bending a long, full-width piece of siding around the outside of the posts, securing it with galvanized screws. Now mount a second length of full-width siding outside the first, alternating the bevel direction from top to bottom. Secure it with screws, yellow water-resistant wood glue, and clamps.

▶ Once the glue is dry, use the upper-rail curves as forms to shape the lower-rail members. Do this by laminating half-width boards together and clamping them to follow the shape of the full-width laminations.

▶ Start by taping a piece of wax paper or plastic wrap around the outer boards, so that the glue used to laminate the pieces will not stick them to the form boards. Next, build up layers of half-width boards, spreading glue on each side and alternating the bevels from top to bottom, until they are the width of the posts. Don't worry about exact length; just make sure the strips extend beyond the posts.

▶ Clamp the built-up rail to the form, using as many clamps as necessary to eliminate gaps between the strips. Then drive screws through the laminations. Be sure not to drive any screw into outer layers you are using as a form.

▶ When the glue dries, remove the lower-rail members, sand them with a belt sander, and cut them to fit between the posts. Attach the lower rails to the post with angled galvanized screws. Now remove the wax paper and finish laminating the top rails. Use half-width pieces over the posts and two full-width pieces inside the curve.

▶ Cut the half-circle, 6-inch-radius bases for the balusters from 2x8 pieces of cedar. Secure them to the lower rails with construction adhesive and galvanized finishing nails.

▶ Mark the positions for the balusters, working outward from the central vertical 2x2. Space the balusters an equal distance apart. Hold each baluster in place to scribe the bottom radius and the angle at its top, then cut them with a saber saw. Mount the balusters with 6d galvanized finishing nails.

▶ Once the railing is complete, install 2x10 rim-joist fascia boards between the 4x4 posts on the straight rim joists. Make sure their tops are flush with the deck's surface. In the same way, cover the curved plywood rim joists with four thicknesses of 1x10 cedar boards planed to a 3/8-inch thickness to enable them to bend. (If you don't own a surface planer, ask your lumberyard to plane the cedar to the required 3/8-inch thickness.) Finally, attach the curved fascias with galvanized screws.

Sanding Tip

As you build the rail laminations, take care in aligning the edges of the siding. The more accurate you are now, the less sanding you'll have to do later.

Railing Posts and Balusters

The top rail is built from full-width, 4-in. beveled cedar. The lower rail is formed of half-width pieces. The end view (far right) shows how the laminated top rail attaches to the posts.

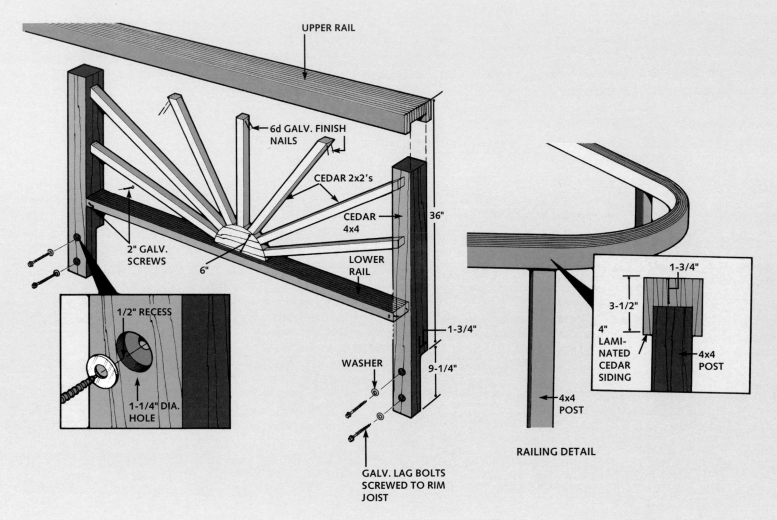

UPPER RAIL

6d GALV. FINISH NAILS

CEDAR 2x2's

CEDAR 4x4

36"

LOWER RAIL

6"

2" GALV. SCREWS

1/2" RECESS

1-1/4" DIA. HOLE

1-3/4"

9-1/4"

WASHER

GALV. LAG BOLTS SCREWED TO RIM JOIST

1-3/4"

3-1/2"

4" LAMI-NATED CEDAR SIDING

4x4 POST

4x4 POST

RAILING DETAIL

Build the Curved Bench

The seat for the curved bench that can be seen at the far left of the photo on page 34 is built much the same way as the railings, using nominal 6-inch beveled cedar siding.

▶ Position the steel support pipes accurately, to achieve smoothly flowing curves. Use a full length of cedar siding as your shaping guide, curving it to form the outer edge of the final shape.

▶ Now determine how wide your bench will be. Measure half of the distance back from the curved edge to locate the support pipes, spacing them evenly about 3 feet apart.

Most of the cedar siding for this bench is composed of half-width strips that rest on top of the 2x4 horizontal supports (see the Curved Bench Detail below and Photo 7). The two thicknesses at the inside and outside edges are full-width strips that cover the ends of the supports.

▶ With yellow wood glue and screws, secure each successive layer of siding to the previous one, alternating the bevels top to bottom. Toenail 1-1/2 inch galvanized finish nails into the horizontal support every few layers to hold the bench top in place. When all the layers are complete, level the high spots with a hand plane and sand the surface smooth with a belt sander.

Photo 7. Assemble the curved bench using 6-in. beveled cedar siding cut in half lengthwise. Use two full-width thicknesses along each outside edge.

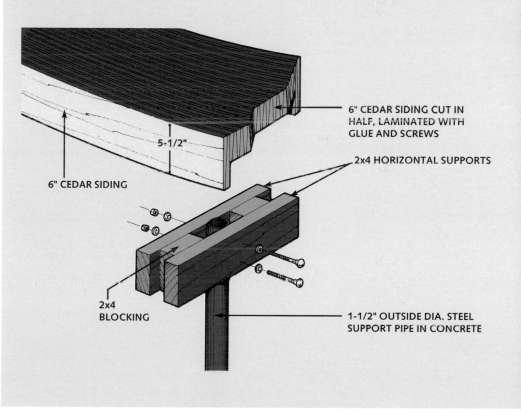

DETAIL

Curved Bench

6" CEDAR SIDING CUT IN HALF, LAMINATED WITH GLUE AND SCREWS

5-1/2"

6" CEDAR SIDING

2x4 HORIZONTAL SUPPORTS

2x4 BLOCKING

1-1/2" OUTSIDE DIA. STEEL SUPPORT PIPE IN CONCRETE

Apply the Finish

When your new deck is finally complete, it's time to decide what kind of finish to apply—or whether to apply any finish at all. Most decks are in fact left unfinished, to weather to a silver-gray color over the years. Bear in mind that finishing is not a one-time activity. You'll need to reapply the finish every two or three years to keep your deck well protected and looking its best.

To minimize the inevitable weathering and extend the life of your deck, choose from two kinds of widely available deck finishes. Clear, water-resistant finishes will darken the wood slightly, but they block water penetration and somewhat reduce sun bleaching. Semitransparent deck stains also reduce water penetration, but they do a better job of minimizing the sun's bleaching because they lay down a colored pigment on the wood's surface.

The deck shown here was treated with a semitransparent latex stain on the railings and bench and a thinner, more transparent penetrating stain of the same color on the deck itself.

TECHNIQUES

Pour a Concrete Patio

This particular deck was designed with a concrete patio adjoining it. The patio should be poured, in two sections, after the deck is in place. An inner section has a washed-stone aggregate surface. The outer, apron, section was set about 1-1/2 inches lower, then covered with thin brick pavers set in a bed of mortar. The concrete for each section is 4 inches thick and is poured on a 2-inch gravel base.

Preparation

Review your patio plans with your local building inspector. Then excavate the entire area to the approved depth and level the surface. Stake the curved form for the inner patio section, then spread a gravel subsurface and tamp it down firmly. Place a fiber expansion joint against the house where the concrete will adjoin it. Keep this expansion joint level, and make sure it is even with the tops of the concrete forms.

When you order your concrete, specify the size and smoothness of the aggregate stones. The concrete used here was small-stone aggregate.

Pouring

Once your concrete is delivered, be prepared to work rapidly. Level the poured concrete with a long board, then smooth it with a steel trowel. After it begins to set up, go over the surface lightly with a wide push broom while applying a fine spray of water to expose the stones in it.

Once the inner section has cured, remove those forms and stake the outer form in place. Pour the concrete so its surface is lower than that of the inner section by an amount equal to the thickness of the brick pavers you'll use for the edging plus about 1/2 inch for the pavers' mortar bed.

For more information about concrete, see Estimating Concrete on page 16.

Backyard Island

Not everyone can own a private island in the Caribbean.

So here's an alternative that's more affordable and more convenient—

a restful island right in your own backyard.

Although most decks are designed to be attached to a house, sometimes the most

appealing place for one is out in the yard, away from household hubbub.

This freestanding deck makes the perfect place to relax or enjoy cold drinks

with family and friends.

This deck has a freestanding, "fits anywhere" design. Its bilevel construction and built-in benches make it enjoyable in many ways.

Plan Your Island Deck

Decide first where you want to place the deck, to take advantage of your yard's slope, sun, shade, view, or breezes.

This freestanding backyard island isn't especially difficult to build, but some stages are a bit tricky. For example, the deck's symmetrical octagonal design makes it essential that you locate the footings precisely. You'll also need to make a lot of angle cuts for the joists, railings, steps, and benches. But if you have above-average do-it-yourself skills and at least some deck or structural building experience, you should be able to build this deck successfully. Plan to spend about 100 hours to complete it.

Building-Code Requirements

Even though this deck will not be attached to your house, your locality may require that you obtain a building permit and have your work inspected. Likewise, although this design fully conforms to national building codes, you may need to make changes to comply with local codes, especially regarding the deck's height above ground level and the design of its railings. Ask a building inspector if there are any special local requirements for footings, railings, or steps.

Tools You'll Need

To build this island, you'll need a standard assortment of hand tools: a hammer, a framing square, an adjustable square, a 3-foot level, a plumb line, a few chisels, and a 20-foot measuring tape. You also should have a heavy-duty 3/8-inch drill (for driving screws as well as drilling holes), a router, and, most important, a good-quality circular saw and sharp blade that will let you make accurate angle and bevel cuts. If you decide to pour concrete footings, you'll need a posthole digger or an 8-inch power auger, which can be rented from a local tool supply outlet if you have a lot of holes to dig.

Although not absolutely necessary, a table saw will be extremely helpful for ripping pieces, notching the railing posts, and cutting the beveled cleats that hold the acrylic plastic side panels in place.

Materials You'll Need

We used pressure-treated lumber for all of the framing members, and cedar for the decking, fascias, railings, steps, and benches. For the 4x4 posts, choose pressure-treated lumber with at least a .40 or "ground contact" designation.

Deck Design Plan

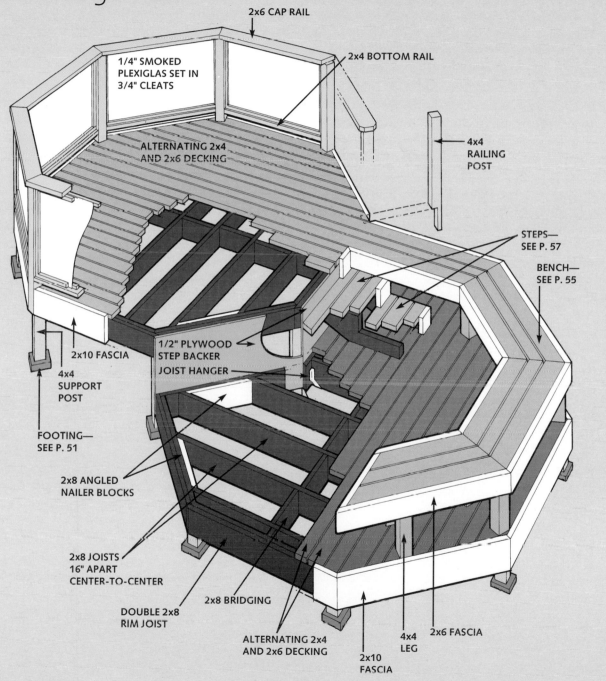

2x6 CAP RAIL

2x4 BOTTOM RAIL

1/4" SMOKED PLEXIGLAS SET IN 3/4" CLEATS

4x4 RAILING POST

ALTERNATING 2x4 AND 2x6 DECKING

STEPS—SEE P. 57

BENCH—SEE P. 55

2x10 FASCIA

1/2" PLYWOOD STEP BACKER

JOIST HANGER

4x4 SUPPORT POST

FOOTING—SEE P. 51

2x8 ANGLED NAILER BLOCKS

2x8 JOISTS 16" APART CENTER-TO-CENTER

DOUBLE 2x8 RIM JOIST

2x8 BRIDGING

ALTERNATING 2x4 AND 2x6 DECKING

2x10 FASCIA

4x4 LEG

2x6 FASCIA

Tools You Need

Hand Tools

Hammer

Framing square

Adjustable square

3-ft. level

Plumb line

Posthole digger

Assorted chisels

20-ft. measuring tape

Nail set

Power Tools

Heavy-duty 3/8-in. drill

Router

Circular saw

Optional

8-in. power auger (rented)

Saber saw

Table saw

Construct Your Island Deck

Lay Out the Deck and Install the Footings

Because this deck isn't attached to a house, you may not be required by code to pour the concrete footings shown in the Footing Layout Plan (right) and Framing and Joist Hanger Details (page 52). In warmer climates, you can use the preformed concrete piers about 6 inches high that are sold at most home centers. Sink the pier bottoms about 2 inches below the soil surface. Any type of footing should rest on firm, undisturbed earth.

If winters are severe where you live, you'll need concrete footings that extend at least 6 inches below the frost line to ensure that your deck won't buckle or sag.

Lay Out the Deck

▶ First lay out the upper-level full octagon. Create a 10-foot square with string and batter boards, as shown in the Footing Layout Plan (right). Adjust the height of the batter boards so the string is level all the way around. Then measure off each of the eight 50-inch sides. This will give you the outside perimeter for the double 2x8 rim joists, as shown in the Top View Framing Detail (page 52).

▶ Now lay out the lower deck, using the same technique of string and batter boards.

Pour the Concrete Footings

If you decide to pour concrete footings, dig holes for them that are slightly wider at the bottom. Build small forms for the tops of the footings by nailing together pieces of 3/4-inch plywood as shown on the facing page. Pack soil firmly around each of the forms to hold them in place while you are pouring the concrete.

Although the tops of the footings must be smooth and level, you don't need to finish all the footings at exactly the same height.

You will be leveling the deck by varying the lengths of its 4x4 support posts. If you build this deck on a slope, the lengths of the support posts will vary considerably. Place a footing under each of the eight points of the string octagon, as shown in the Footing Layout Plan on the facing page.

While the concrete is still wet, set 6-inch lengths of 1/4-inch galvanized steel rod 4 inches into the footings to serve as drift pins. Although these pins are not essential, they will help secure the deck on its footings. Bevel the footing tops slightly to shed water. A good footing will also be wider at the bottom and narrower toward the top, to avoid frost heaves. For examples of well-made footings, see Build a Solid Foundation on pages 16–17.

Footing Layout Plan

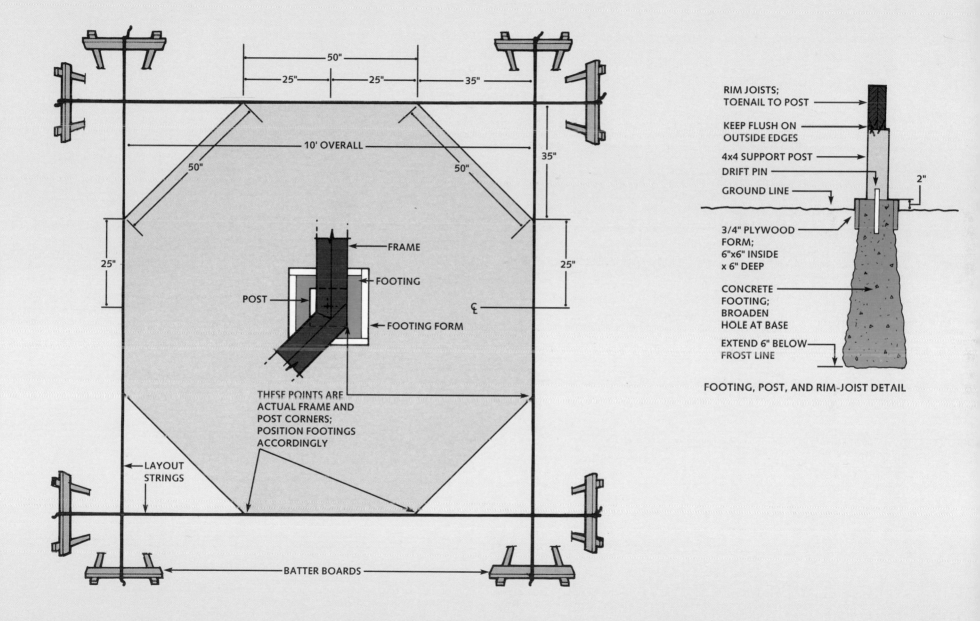

50"

25" 25" 35"

10' OVERALL

35"

50" 50"

25" 25"

FRAME

FOOTING

POST

FOOTING FORM

THESE POINTS ARE
ACTUAL FRAME AND
POST CORNERS;
POSITION FOOTINGS
ACCORDINGLY

LAYOUT
STRINGS

BATTER BOARDS

RIM JOISTS;
TOENAIL TO POST

KEEP FLUSH ON
OUTSIDE EDGES

4x4 SUPPORT POST

DRIFT PIN

GROUND LINE

2"

3/4" PLYWOOD
FORM;
6"x6" INSIDE
x 6" DEEP

CONCRETE
FOOTING;
BROADEN
HOLE AT BASE

EXTEND 6" BELOW
FROST LINE

FOOTING, POST, AND RIM-JOIST DETAIL

Framing and Joist Hanger

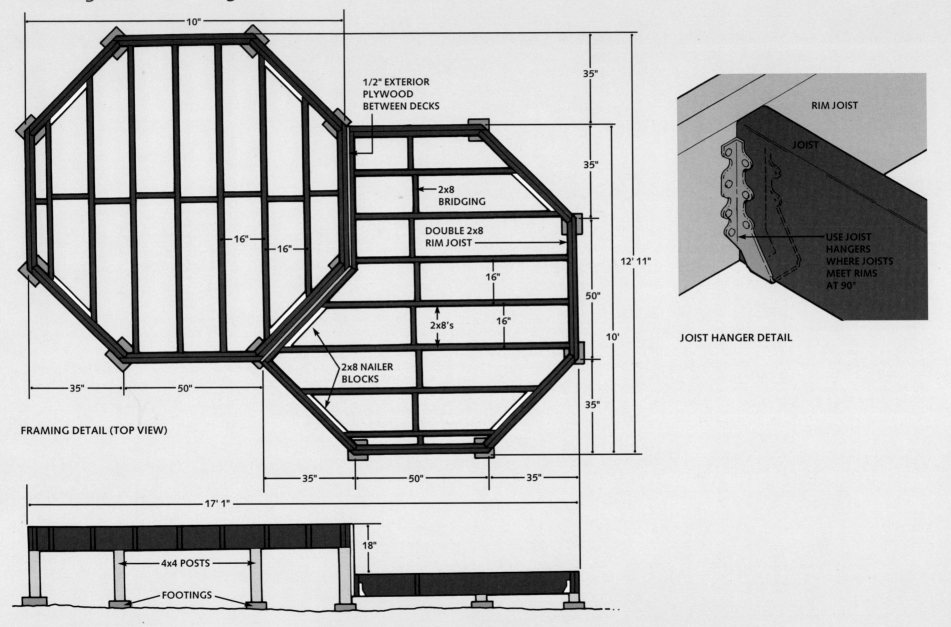

10"

35"

1/2" EXTERIOR
PLYWOOD
BETWEEN DECKS

35"

2x8
BRIDGING

DOUBLE 2x8
RIM JOIST

16"

16"

16"

50"

12' 11"

16"

2x8's

16"

10'

2x8 NAILER
BLOCKS

35"

35"

50"

FRAMING DETAIL (TOP VIEW)

35"   50"   35"

RIM JOIST

JOIST

USE JOIST
HANGERS
WHERE JOISTS
MEET RIMS
AT 90°

JOIST HANGER DETAIL

17' 1"

18"

4x4 POSTS

FOOTINGS

FRAMING DETAIL (SIDE VIEW)

Build the Framing

Check the batter boards and restring them, if they've been knocked askew, to reestablish the exact positions of the posts. All eight posts must be flush with the outside rim-joist perimeter to avoid trouble later when you attach the 2x10 fascia boards.

Cut and Install the Support Posts

▶ Cut the 4x4 deck-support posts to length, starting with the shortest post on the lower deck. Work your way from footing to footing with a level taped to a straight 12-foot length of 2x4. Measure and cut each succeeding post to the proper length so that it is level with the first one. Follow the same procedure to measure and cut each of the support posts for the upper deck.

▶ Drill 1/4-inch drift-pin holes 2 inches deep into the centers of the post bottoms, then set the posts on the pins.

Build the Upper Rim-Joist Assembly

Begin by cutting the outer rim-joist pieces for the upper deck.

▶ First cut four of the eight outside rim-joist pieces, with 45-degree bevels on each end cut at opposite angles as shown in the top Framing Detail (left). Make the distance from one inside angle point to another (the "short side" measure) 50 inches.

▶ Lay these pieces on the post tops to form four opposing sides. Adjust their position so that each of the eight sides will measure 50 inches long, again from inside angle to inside angle. Then make sure that the 50-inch lengths needed for the other four

outside rim-joist pieces are correct and cut them to length, with opposing 45-degree bevels at each end as shown in the Top View Framing Detail at the left.

▶ Set the eight outer rim-joist pieces in place on the posts and drill pilot holes to assemble the octagon with 3-inch deck screws. After it is assembled, toenail the rim joists to the tops of the posts with galvanized nails as shown in the Footing, Post, and Rim-Joist Detail (page 51).

Finish Framing the Upper Deck

Frame the rest of the upper-deck octagon.

▶ Measure and cut the ends of the inner rim joists at 22-1/2 degree angles. All eight will be the same length. Attach them to the outer rim joists' 4x4 posts with 16d galvanized nails.

▶ Measure and cut the long internal 2x8 joists. Where joists join each other at 90-degree angles, use galvanized joist hangers for further strength, as shown in the top right detail (left). Where joists meet at a 45-degree angle, nail 45-degree bevel-cut 2x8 nailer blocks inside the rim joists, as shown in the Deck Design Plan (page 49) and the Top View Framing Detail (left). Nail the joist ends in place against the blocks using 16d galvanized nails.

▶ Measure and cut 2x8 bridging to fit between the internal joists, as shown in the Top View Framing Detail. This bridging will keep the joists from bowing or twisting out of position and will strengthen the deck.

Install the bridging between the joists so that adjacent pieces are offset. Then nail through the joists into the ends of the bridging, again with 16d galvanized nails.

Frame the Lower Deck

Build the lower deck's framing following the same procedure you used for the upper deck. Note, however, that the lower deck has only a single rim joist at the point where it joins the upper deck.

▶ Attach the two deck levels with 1/2-inch pressure-treated plywood (Photo 1) as shown in the Deck Design Plan on page 49. Then drive 16d galvanized nails through the lower-deck rim joist and plywood into the 4x4 support posts behind them.

Photo 1. This double-octagon deck frame is built with pressure-treated lumber for the framing members and cedar for decking and other visible parts. Double 2x8 rim joists rest on 4x4 support posts and support the 2x8 joists. The decks are joined by 1/2-in. plywood sheets.

Lay the Deck and Bench Boards

Deck boards, especially 2x6's, are prone to cupping, with one side—the side that originally faced the tree's bark—slightly convex and the other, inner, side slightly concave. This curvature, which can be seen in the growth rings on a board's end grain, gets more and more pronounced as the board weathers. To promote good drainage and prevent rot, always lay deck boards with the convex side facing up.

Start with the Lower Deck
Lay the boards on the lower deck first.
▶ Alternate 2x4's and 2x6's as shown in the Decking Plan (opposite) and secure them with two 3-inch deck screws per joist. Drive them at a slight angle for maximum strength. Set all screw heads about 1/16 inch below the wood's surface. Drilling pilot holes will eliminate splitting and make the screwdriving easier.
▶ If you prefer, you can use 16d galvanized nails instead of screws. Nailing won't take as long, but nails also won't grip as well as screws. When you drive nails, leave the heads slightly above the surface of the deck so you won't dimple the wood with the hammer. Then go over the entire surface with a nail set after you've laid all the decking, setting the heads 1/16 inch below the wood's surface.
▶ As you lay the deck boards, let any long ends overhang the rim joists. After all the decking is in place, mark the the boards by

snapping a chalk line flush with the outside rim joist, then cut off the ends at the line with a circular saw.
▶ For drainage, leave a 1/8-inch gap—about the diameter of a 16d nail, which makes a convenient spacer—between the deck boards. This spacing has been allowed for in the dimensions of the bench shown in the Decking Detail on the facing page.

Lay the Upper-Deck Boards
Some of the bench seating boards are extensions of the upper deck's flooring boards (Photo 2). To support these boards while you lay the decking on the upper level, build at least one pair of 4x4 bench legs and tack them temporarily in place on the lower deck as shown in the bench detail. These extended upper-deck boards should be about 16 feet long. Cut their bench ends at a 22-1/2 degree angle.

Photo 2. Some of the upper-deck boards—alternating cedar 2x4's and 2x6's—extend to form the first section of the bench on the lower deck.

Align the point of the outside board with the point of the rim joist below as shown in the Bench Detail on the facing page.

Complete the Bench
Build the remaining bench legs from 4x4's and 2x4's as shown in the Bench Detail.
▶ Position the first three sets of bench legs directly at the lower-deck corners and at a 22-1/2 degree angle to the sides, as shown in the Deck Design Plan (page 49) and the Bench Detail (right). Toenail the bench legs to the deck boards with small-headed 16d galvanized casing nails.
▶ Measure, cut, and fit the bench boards one bench section at a time, using 10d galvanized casing nails as fasteners. Angle the board ends at 22-1/2 degrees. Position each outside bench board point directly on top of a rim-joist point. Maintain an equal 1/8 inch of spacing between the boards.
▶ Temporarily position the fourth set of bench legs while you cut and fit the fourth section of bench boards. Once everything is aligned, nail the boards and legs in place. Wait to install the bench fascia boards until the whole deck is completed, so that you can add the deck, step, and bench fascias all at the same time.

Decking Plan

Bench Plan

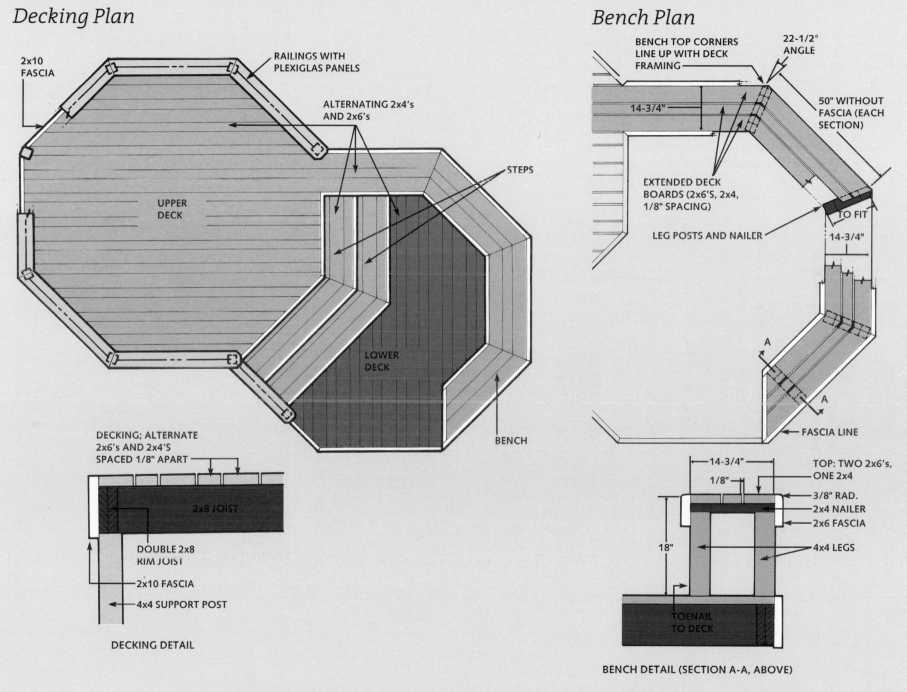

Decking Plan labels:

2x10 FASCIA

RAILINGS WITH PLEXIGLAS PANELS

ALTERNATING 2x4's AND 2x6's

UPPER DECK

STEPS

LOWER DECK

BENCH

DECKING; ALTERNATE 2x6's AND 2x4'S SPACED 1/8" APART

2x8 JOIST

DOUBLE 2x8 RIM JOIST

2x10 FASCIA

4x4 SUPPORT POST

DECKING DETAIL

Bench Plan labels:

BENCH TOP CORNERS LINE UP WITH DECK FRAMING

22-1/2° ANGLE

14-3/4"

50" WITHOUT FASCIA (EACH SECTION)

EXTENDED DECK BOARDS (2x6'S, 2x4, 1/8" SPACING)

TO FIT

LEG POSTS AND NAILER

14-3/4"

A

A

FASCIA LINE

14-3/4"

1/8"

18"

TOP: TWO 2x6's, ONE 2x4

3/8" RAD.

2x4 NAILER

2x6 FASCIA

4x4 LEGS

TOENAIL TO DECK

BENCH DETAIL (SECTION A-A, ABOVE)

Build the Steps and Railing Posts

Take extra care building the long, angled steps of this deck, because they are a main focal point for this project.

Cut the Outside Step Stringers

Cut the four outermost step stringers from a length of 2x12, using the dimensions in the Stringer Detail (right). Toenail the stringers securely to the deck boards, through the 1/2-inch plywood and into the 4x4 support posts behind. Where there's no support post, drive 3-inch deck screws through the plywood from behind into the back edge of the stringer.

Cut the Step Boards and Center Stringer

▶ Cut all the boards for each step—two 2x4's with a 2x6 in between. Cut one end of each board at a 22-1/2 degree angle where the boards meet at the center of the steps (Photo 3). Then lay the boards in place, but do not nail them yet. Allow the other ends of the boards to extend beyond the outside stringers. Place 16d nails between the boards to maintain an even 1/8-inch of spacing between them.

▶ When all the step boards have been properly positioned, measure the tread depth at the location of the center stringer. You may need to remove a few boards to get accurate

dimensions. Cut the center stringer (see the Stringer Detail, right) to size, making 22-1/2 degree bevels where the risers will be attached (see Steps Plan, right). Toenail the center stringer in place.

▶ Reposition all the step boards. Mark and trim the long board ends flush with the outside stringers, then nail the step boards in place, maintaining an even 1/8-inch spacing.

Cut and Install the Risers

Cut down 2x8's to 6 inches wide for the two risers. Cut one end of each riser at a 22-1/2 degree angle where the risers meet at the center of the steps. Fit the risers in place, then mark the ends so they are flush with the outer stringers. Cut the risers to size and nail them into position.

Photo 3. The upper deck is 18 in. higher than the lower level, with 6-in. steps connecting the two. Each tread consists of 2x4's flanking a 2x6.

Cut and Mount the Railing Posts

Three of the deck's eight railing posts mount flat against the rim joists. Cut flush notches into their lower ends, as shown in the Flush-Notched Post Detail on page 59. Start the cuts with a circular saw or table saw and finish them with a handsaw.

The remaining five railing posts mount at the points of the upper deck, letting the railing follow the octagonal shape of the deck. This requires making beveled notches in the posts, as shown in the Bevel-Notched Post Details on page 59.

▶ To make the beveled notches, set the blade of a table saw at 67-1/2 degrees and make the two vertical bevels shown in the diagram. Then make the horizontal cut to the same depth as the vertical cuts. The round saw blade will have left some uncut wood at the point of the notch and below the horizontal cut, which you will have to remove using a sharp 1-1/2 inch chisel.

▶ Locate and drill 14 7/16-inch clearance holes for the 3/8-inch lag screws, and 5/8-inch deep counterbore holes 1 inch in diameter to recess the washers and screw heads. Drill 1/4-inch pilot holes and mount each post in place with a few angled deck screws, as shown in the Railing Posts and Fascia Diagram on page 59. Use a level to double-check that all of the posts are perfectly vertical, and then secure them with the lag screws and washers.

Steps Plan and Details

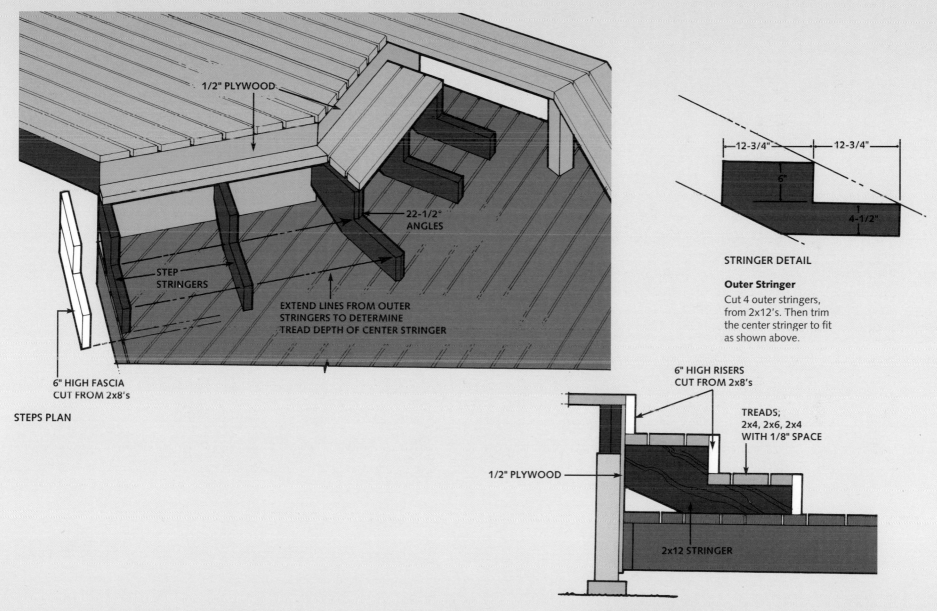

1/2" PLYWOOD

22-1/2°
ANGLES

STEP
STRINGERS

EXTEND LINES FROM OUTER
STRINGERS TO DETERMINE
TREAD DEPTH OF CENTER STRINGER

6" HIGH FASCIA
CUT FROM 2x8's

STEPS PLAN

12-3/4"   12-3/4"

6"

4-1/2"

STRINGER DETAIL

Outer Stringer

Cut 4 outer stringers,
from 2x12's. Then trim
the center stringer to fit
as shown above.

6" HIGH RISERS
CUT FROM 2x8's

TREADS;
2x4, 2x6, 2x4
WITH 1/8" SPACE

1/2" PLYWOOD

2x12 STRINGER

STEPS CROSS SECTION

Attach the Fascias and Railings

The last phase before applying the finishing touches is to enclose the perimeter of the deck with fascias, railings, and acrylic clear plastic paneling such as the Plexiglas used in this project.

Add the Deck, Step, and Bench Fascias

▶ Measure, cut, and fit the 2x10 fascias between the railing posts, around the perimeter of each deck, as shown in the Railing Posts and Fascia Diagram (right). Attach the fascias with 16d galvanized casing nails. Use a nail set to sink the heads slightly below the wood surface.

▶ Measure and cut 6-inch wide fascias from 2x8's for the sides of the steps. Nail them to the outside of the step stringers, as shown in the Steps Plan on page 57.

▶ Cut the 2x6 fascias to size for the edges of the bench, as shown in the Bench Detail on page 55. Make 22-1/2 degree bevel cuts at each joint, and then nail the fascias to the bench boards and legs with 16d galvanized casing nails.

Add the Railings

▶ Measure and cut the 2x6 cap rails, beveling the ends as shown in the Deck Design Plan on page 49 and the Railings and Acrylic Plastic Paneling diagrams on page 60. Cut and fit one cap-rail section at a time, checking each one with a level to make sure each post is vertical. Then secure the cap rails to the tops of the posts using 3-inch galvanized deck screws.

▶ Measure and cut the 2x4 bottom rails that fit between each pair of posts, and secure them with angled 3-inch deck screws. The ends of the angle-cut 2x4's will be wider than the 4x4 posts; let them extend to the outside of the posts. Shape and sand the points flush with the posts as shown in Detail 3 on page 60.

▶ Trial and error will produce the double-angled notch where the handrail attaches to the railing post (Photos 4 and 5). Start with a 2x6 that's at least a foot longer than you'll need, so you can start over if you make a mistake. Lay out the shape of the notch first, then mark the appropriate angle and cut it out with a handsaw or saber saw. Attach the handrails with 3-inch galvanized deck screws. Bevel the top of the lower post to the same angle as the railing.

ATTACH THE FASCIAS AND RAILINGS

Photo 4. The deck railings are 4x4 support posts topped with 2x6 cap rails. Joining the handrails to their posts requires cutting a tricky double-angled notch.

Photo 5. Cut the railing panels from 1/4-in. acrylic sheeting (here Plexiglas), using a carbide-tip blade. Cut slowly with a straightedge to avoid chipping.

Railing Posts and Fascia

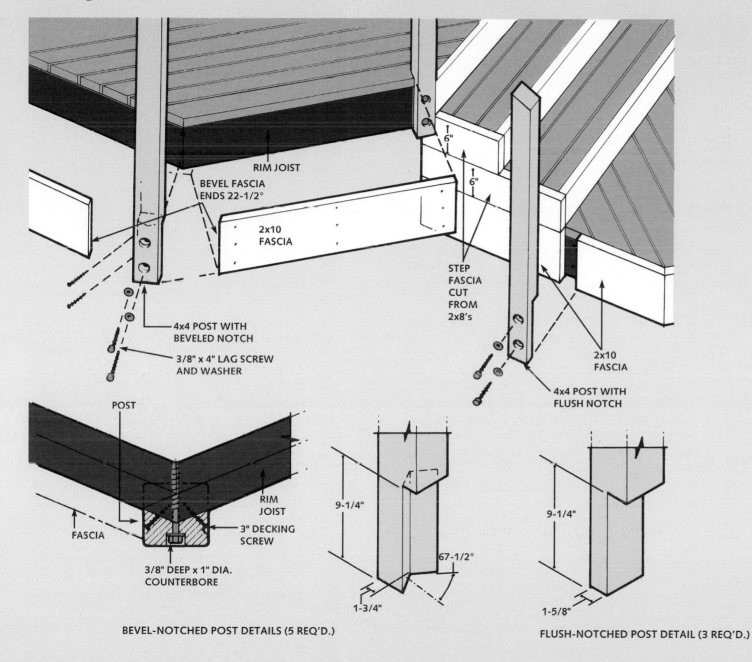

RIM JOIST

BEVEL FASCIA
ENDS 22-1/2°

2x10
FASCIA

6"

6"

STEP
FASCIA
CUT
FROM
2x8's

4x4 POST WITH
BEVELED NOTCH

3/8" x 4" LAG SCREW
AND WASHER

2x10
FASCIA

4x4 POST WITH
FLUSH NOTCH

POST

RIM
JOIST

FASCIA

3" DECKING
SCREW

3/8" DEEP x 1" DIA.
COUNTERBORE

BEVEL-NOTCHED POST DETAILS (5 REQ'D.)

9-1/4"

67-1/2°

1-3/4"

9-1/4"

1-5/8"

FLUSH-NOTCHED POST DETAIL (3 REQ'D.)

Toenailing Tip

It's often necessary in deck building to toenail two frame members together. A couple of techniques will make it easy. First blunt the nail by tapping its end, so the wood won't split when you nail near the end. Then start the nail 1/3 of its length from the post's end, at a 45-degree angle. Finish with a nail set.

Railings and Acrylic Plastic Paneling

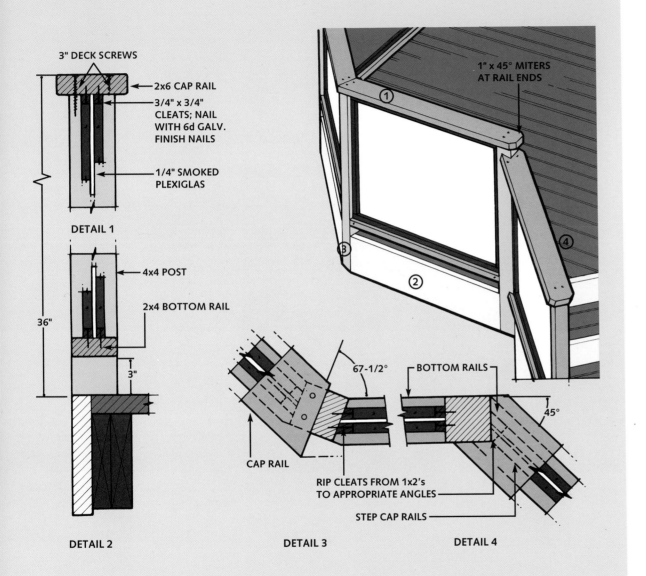

3" DECK SCREWS

2x6 CAP RAIL

3/4" x 3/4" CLEATS; NAIL WITH 6d GALV. FINISH NAILS

1/4" SMOKED PLEXIGLAS

DETAIL 1

4x4 POST

2x4 BOTTOM RAIL

36"

3"

DETAIL 2

1" x 45° MITERS AT RAIL ENDS

① ③ ② ④

67-1/2°

BOTTOM RAILS

45°

CAP RAIL

RIP CLEATS FROM 1x2's TO APPROPRIATE ANGLES

STEP CAP RAILS

DETAIL 3

DETAIL 4

Add the Finishing Touches

Now all that remains before you can begin enjoying your new backyard island is to install acrylic paneling on the sides and then sand and apply a finish.

Install the Acrylic Paneling

The panels shown are 1/4-inch smoked Plexiglas, commonly available at glass retailers or at dealers listed under "Plastics" in the Yellow Pages.

▶ Measure the railing openings, then cut the panels 1/8-inch smaller in each direction to allow for expansion and contraction by the wood and Plexiglas. With the protective paper covering still in place, cut the panels on a table saw, or use a circular saw with a straight board clamped in place to serve as a guide. In either case, be sure to use a sharp, carbide-tip blade and cut slowly, to avoid chipping the edges. Smooth all the edges with medium (60–100 grit) and then fine (120–180 grit) sandpaper before you begin installing the panels.

▶ Use a table saw to rip 1x2's into cleats 3/4-inch square to hold the panels in place, as shown in Detail 1 (left). Angle-cut the ends of the cleats as necessary as seen in Detail 3. Bevel the back faces of the vertical cleats so their inside faces align with those of the adjacent horizontal cleats.

▶ Install galvanized 6d finish nails every 4 to 6 inches. Install the outer cleats first, then position the panels (Photo 6). Finally, install the inside cleats (Photo 7).

Sand the Deck

Round-over all the outer edges of the bench fascias with a router fitted with a 3/8-inch round-over bit (Photo 8). Be sure also to round-over the pointed ends of the bench fascias, to avoid injuries. Then do the same thing to the top edges of the cap rails.

Sand all the rough edges of the deck with coarse (36–50 grit) sandpaper. Next, sand off any dirty spots, footprints, and lumber-grading stamps that remain visible.

Apply a Finish

Apply a good-quality transparent deck finish designed to block penetration by both sun and water. Check the label of the finish you intend to apply to make sure it's recommended specifically for the lumber you've used. Apply the finish with a brush or a lamb's-wool applicator.

Finally, if you like, grade the soil around the deck to tie it in with the lower level. You especially may find it desirable to grade the approach to the lower deck. The first step up from the ground will be a lot more comfortable for most people if this rise is 8 inches or less. Once that's done, carry up your favorite chair and enjoy the view from your new backyard getaway.

ADD THE FINISHING TOUCHES

Photo 6. Position the acrylic-plastic panels between the posts and rails after smoothing the panels' edges with medium, then fine, sandpaper. Mount the panels with cleats cut from cedar 1x2's.

Photo 7. Cut bevels on the vertical retainer cleats so that the inside faces of each of the cleats will align all the way around. Then attach the cleats, using 6d galvanized nails.

Photo 8. Round-over the top edges of the benches and cap rails, using a 3/8-in. round-over bit. Be especially careful to round-over any sharp points at the ends of the benches.

Bilevel Pool Deck

Combining a deck with a pool can bring out the best of both.

A deck not only provides easy access to the pool but also helps it blend into the landscape

of your backyard. And the shade created by the optional arbor, or pergola,

may be very welcome in the heat of the summer.

A well-designed deck can make an above-ground pool look as good as a more elaborate—and expensive—in-ground pool. And the deck railing here doubles as a built-in safety fence.

Construction Plan

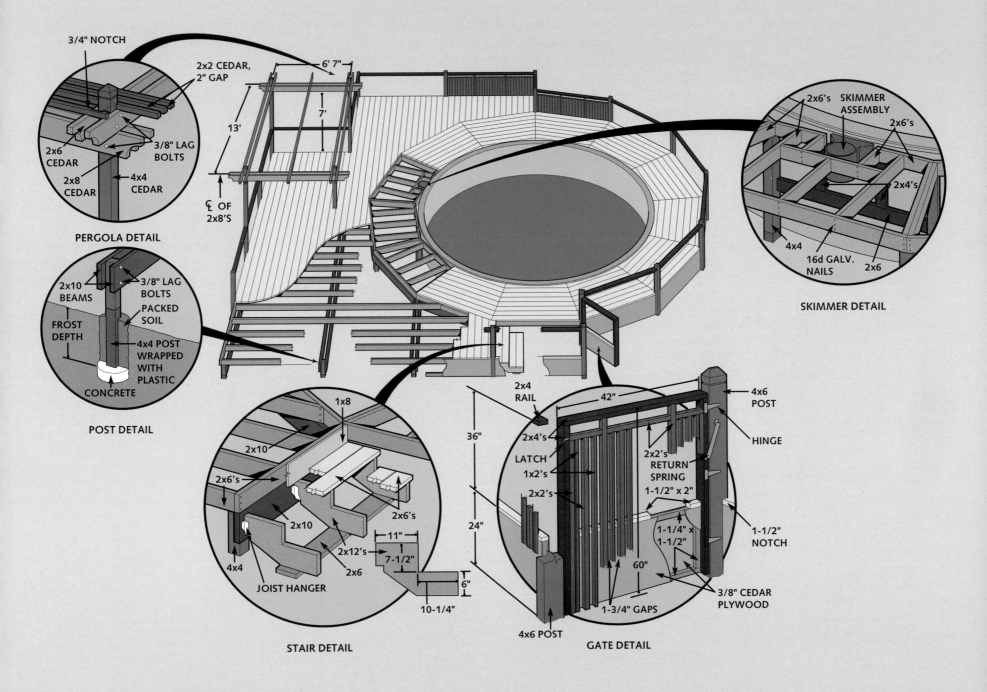

3/4" NOTCH

2x2 CEDAR, 2" GAP

2x6 CEDAR

2x8 CEDAR

3/8" LAG BOLTS

4x4 CEDAR

PERGOLA DETAIL

6' 7"

7'

13'

℄ OF 2x8'S

2x10 BEAMS

3/8" LAG BOLTS

PACKED SOIL

FROST DEPTH

4x4 POST WRAPPED WITH PLASTIC

CONCRETE

POST DETAIL

2x6's SKIMMER ASSEMBLY

2x6's

2x4's

4x4

16d GALV. NAILS

2x6

SKIMMER DETAIL

1x8

2x10

2x6's

2x6's

2x10

2x12's

2x6

4x4

JOIST HANGER

11"

7-1/2"

6"

10-1/4"

STAIR DETAIL

2x4 RAIL

36"

24"

2x4's

LATCH

1x2's

2x2's

42"

2x2's

RETURN SPRING

1-1/2" x 2"

60"

4x6 POST

HINGE

1-1/2" NOTCH

1-1/4" x 1-1/2"

3/8" CEDAR PLYWOOD

4x6 POST

1-3/4" GAPS

GATE DETAIL

Plan Your Pool Deck

This particular freestanding deck was built well away from the house, but you could just as easily connect it to the house to make the pool and deck even more accessible.

Size Considerations

This deck is a big, statement-making addition to your property. Its large size dramatically demonstrates how attractive an aboveground pool and deck combination can be, but this design may prove too big for your backyard. If that's the case, you can either opt for a smaller-size pool or reduce the size of the attached rectangular deck.

A typical aboveground pool has a flat bottom and is uniformly 42 to 48 inches deep. Its sides rise anywhere from 2 to 4 feet above the ground, depending on whether there's a slope where it's installed.

Time and Skill Considerations

The pool's curvature is what provides the real building challenge. This project utilizes the entire arsenal of tricks that experienced builders use to build circular decks. Don't attempt it unless you've already laid out, framed, and built conventionally designed decks. Building the deck itself is likely to take your spare time for a summer unless you can recruit help or pay the pros to do some of the heavy-duty work like digging the postholes and setting the posts. But if you're ready for a real building challenge,

the payoff can be satisfying. This chapter assumes you have good basic building skills, so some elementary procedures are not detailed. But it will show you some of the finer points and provide insider tips that will help you complete it like a pro. (For a review of deck-building basics not covered here, see "Deck Builder's Companion," pages 12–21.)

Although this deck design is admittedly complicated, it will help if you break it down into its three main parts: the curved 4-foot walkway surrounding the pool, the rectangular adjoining deck, and the railing.

Building the curved walkway will most likely challenge even professional builders. For the best results, lay it out using a lot of 4x4 posts so the decking is supported right up to the edge of the pool. This deck incorporates a deck post at each of the pool's own frame posts for a total of thirteen, so the framing hugs the sides of the pool.

Pool Considerations

The pool shown on these pages came with an attractive hard plastic cap around its top edge that was strong enough to walk on. If your pool has something similar, don't cover it with the walkway. Instead, extend the decking right up against it, leaving no more than a 1/4-inch gap. Otherwise, you may want to adapt this design to run the decking over the top frame edges of your pool. Ask your pool dealer for advice.

Safety Factors

Adhere closely to your local building codes to make your pool and deck as safe as they can be. Local regulations vary and may specify other safety measures not shown here, especially regarding protective fences, latching, and barriers. Talk to your local building inspector during the planning stage and be sure to obtain any necessary building permits for both the deck and the pool.

Although you can design the rectangular portion of your deck just as you would any other deck with right angles (see, for example, "Showcase Deck" on pages 22–33), the railing around the deck and pool requires special attention. Typically, a deck railing should be at least 36 inches high, with baluster openings no wider than 4 inches. However, most building codes require a 4-foot barrier around the pool, with no openings larger than 1-3/4 inches.

Since this deck railing also serves as the pool barrier, it uses this narrower spacing between balusters to comply with the stricter regulations for pools. The lower part of the barrier is the plywood skirting that conceals the deck framing. Code regulations for pool barriers can be complex, so always obtain your building inspector's approval of your plans before beginning to work.

Tools You Need

Hand Tools

Angle finder or speed square

Chalk line

50-ft. measuring tape

2' or 4' level

Plumb bob

Posthole digger

Pry bar

Ratchet wrench

Water level

Power Tools

Circular saw

Drill

8-in. auger (2-person)

Jigsaw

Optional

Drill with screwdriver blades

Construct Your Pool Deck

Lay Out, Set, and Trim the Posts

The following sequence shows the key building steps, techniques, and details involved in completing this project.

Laying Out the Post Locations

It's best to decide now whether you will want to add the shading pergola. If so, make three of the rectangular platform's outside posts extra-long (see the Pergola Detail in the Construction Plan on page 64).

▶ To lay out the post locations for the circular walkway as shown in the Framing and Dimensions Diagram on the facing page, first find the pool's center (Photo 1). To do this, hook one end of a 50-foot measuring tape over a nail driven in the center of a 20-foot 2x6 and lay the 2x6 across the middle of the pool. (Nail together two shorter 2x6's if you can't find one long enough.) To stabilize the 2x6, nail a 10-foot 2x4 to it at a 90-degree angle. Now walk around the pool, measuring to the pool edge and shifting the 2x6 until all measurements are as nearly equal as possible. Your various measurements probably won't be identical, because the pool won't be perfectly round.

▶ If you live in a region where the ground freezes, carefully position the posts that are closest to the pool. You don't want the 2x6 framing that will run between them to extend under the pool edge, where frost heaves could cause damage to the pool.

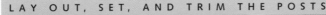

LAY OUT, SET, AND TRIM THE POSTS

Photo 1. Find the locations for the walkway posts with a measuring tape stretched from the center of the pool as explained in the text, directly over the top of each pool post. Drop a plumb bob to mark the spot.

Photo 2. Position 4x4 pressure-treated posts, using a measuring tape or string lines. Plumb the posts with a level, and then tamp the soil in firmly around them with a scrap piece of 2x4.

Photo 3. Using one post as a reference, mark the correct height for each of the other posts using a water level. Then trim each of the posts to its final length with a circular saw.

Setting the Posts

▶ Rent an 8-inch, two-person power auger to drill the postholes. You'll also need a hand posthole digger to clean out the holes. For rocky soil, a 5-foot pry bar will also come in handy. In a northern climate, you may have to dig down 48 inches or more to reach below the frost line.

▶ Take extra care when digging holes alongside the pool. To avoid damaging the sides of the pool with the power auger, dig or at least finish these holes by hand.

▶ Mix a half-sack of concrete with water and pour it into each hole for a footing (see the Post Detail on page 64; for more footings see page 17). Make sure the footing holes are wider at the bottom than at the top.

▶ To protect your 4x4 posts from rot, buy posts treated with preservative to the .60 level (rated for foundations) rather than the .40 level (rated for ground contact).

▶ If your soil is clay and is susceptible to frost, staple heavy plastic sheeting around the posts to keep frost from grabbing them and heaving them upward in winter.

▶ Position the posts carefully, using string lines and a level (Photo 2). Accurate work now will make the rest of your job easier.

▶ Note where you'll want the holes for the 4x6 gate posts, but dig them later.

Trimming the Posts

▶ There are two ways to cut the support posts to their final height: rent a transit to mark the height on each post, or else use water level attachments on a garden hose (Photo 3). Whichever method you use, mark the cutting lines, then make the cuts with a circular saw, finishing with a handsaw.

DIAGRAM

Framing and Dimensions

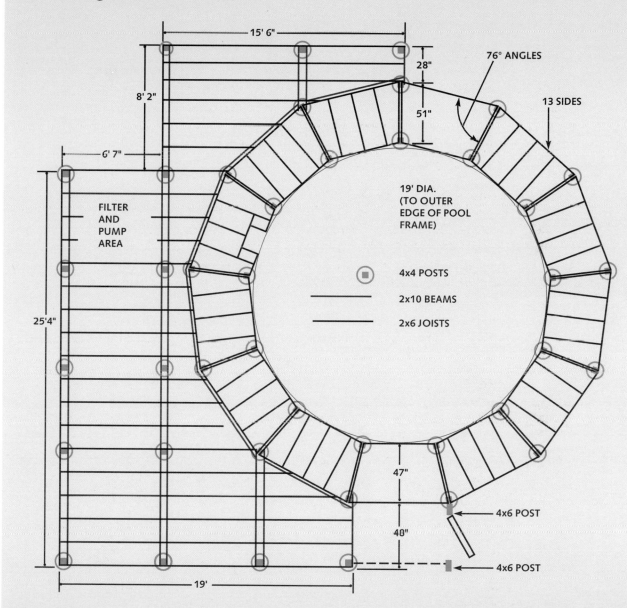

15' 6"

28"

76° ANGLES

8' 2"

51"

13 SIDES

6' 7"

19' DIA.
(TO OUTER
EDGE OF POOL
FRAME)

FILTER
AND
PUMP
AREA

25'4"

■ 4x4 POSTS

——— 2x10 BEAMS

——— 2x6 JOISTS

47"

40"

4x6 POST

19'

4x6 POST

Frame the Walkway and Deck

Now you are ready to frame out the circular walkway and attached rectangular deck, referring to the Framing and Dimensions Diagram on page 67.

Framing the Walkway

▶ Because your pool probably isn't perfectly round, the individual sections of 2x6 framing that enclose it won't be identical in size. Build the sections one at a time, measuring each board individually and cutting it to its proper length (Photo 4). Nail the sections together with 16d galvanized nails.

▶ The walkway section that will house the pool's skimmer equipment will require some special framing (see the Skimmer Detail on page 64).

▶ Add stairs by modifying the measurements in the Stair Detail (page 64) to fit your deck. For more information on stairs see "Backyard Island" (pages 56–57).

Framing the Deck

▶ Use pressure-treated lumber for all framing members (Photo 5).

▶ Let the beams and joists run slightly long. When all the framing is complete, snap a chalk line and cut the ends off all at once, to form perfectly straight sides (Photo 6).

Drilling Tip

Using an extra-long 3/8 in. diameter drill bit will make it easier to bore the many deep holes that are required for this project.

NOT UNDER EDGE OF POOL

2x6 FRAMING SECTION

Photo 4. Measure each walkway unit individually, then cut and nail the 2x6 framing members together. Nail the walkway sections onto the post tops.

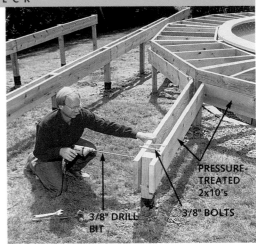

PRESSURE-TREATED 2x10's

3/8" DRILL BIT

3/8" BOLTS

Photo 5. Tack the 2x10 beams to the posts with 16d nails. Then drill 15/64-in. pilot holes and bolt them in place with 3/8-in. carriage bolts.

CUT ENDS LATER

2x6 JOISTS

2x10

Photo 6. Lay out the 2x6 joists 16 in. on center and toenail them to the beams. Rest one end of each joist on a 2x10 fastened to the perimeter.

TECHNIQUES
Calculating and Cutting Angles

To compute the angles at which to cut the framing members, divide 360 degrees by the number of pool walkway support posts you've set (see the Framing and Dimensions Diagram on page 67), then divide that result by 2 and subtract the total from 90 degrees. This particular walkway had 13 support posts and thus required a cutting angle of 76 degrees (360 ÷ 13 = 28 ÷ 2 = 14; 90 - 14 = 76).

Add the Decking and Skirting

Once the walkway and deck are framed out, follow the steps below to lay the decking and install the outside skirting.

Laying the Decking

▶ Lay the 2x6 cedar deck boards, using 16d nails as spacers between them (Photo 7). Nail the ends of any bowed boards first, then force the bowed part against the previous row. Finally, drive a wide wooden shim between the rows to space the bowed boards properly.

▶ Predrill screw holes near board edges so the decking won't split when you drive the 3-inch galvanized screws (Photo 8).

▶ Lay the 2x8 or 2x10 boards adjacent to the pool edge as the last step in each section. Scribe the curve of the pool edge (Photo 8).

▶ Install 2x6 blocking boards to support the ends of the deck boards where they meet the perimeter of the walkway (Photo 9).

▶ Allow a 3/8-inch overlap at all deck edges, to cover the top edges of the 3/8-inch cedar plywood skirting that you'll add next.

Installing the Skirting

Now stain and install the skirting pieces.

▶ To allow for better ventilation under the deck, consider omitting the skirting on the side of the deck that faces away from the house. Instead, continue the railing 2x2's all the way to the ground.

▶ When building this deck on a slope, place the pump and filter equipment for the most clearance. This design allowed access under a section with a 4-foot clearance by using a removable section of 2x2's (Photo 10).

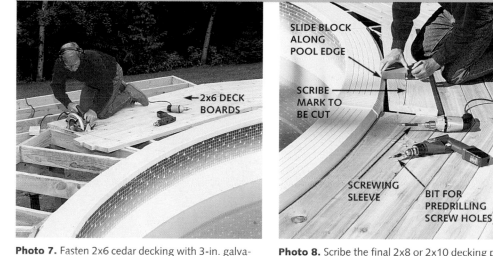

Photo 7. Fasten 2x6 cedar decking with 3-in. galvanized screws. Let the ends run long, then trim all those in one section at once.

Photo 8. Scribe the final 2x8 or 2x10 decking piece to fit the curve of the pool, leaving a 1/4-in. space. Cut the curve with a jigsaw and screw the board into place.

Photo 9. Screw the rest of the deck boards to the joists. Lay the first board at the outer edge of the walkway, then work out from it in both directions.

Photo 10. Fasten pressure-treated 2x4 backing to the posts and screw on the 3/8-in. cedar plywood skirting. Stain the skirting before installing it.

Caution

If your pool uses a gas-fueled heater, do not install it underneath the deck. The combination of wood and gas fuel can present a fire risk.

Railing Design

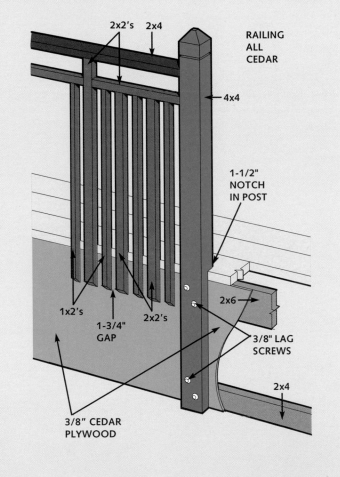

2x2's 2x4

RAILING
ALL
CEDAR

4x4

1-1/2"
NOTCH
IN POST

1x2's

1-3/4"
GAP

2x2's

2x6

3/8" LAG
SCREWS

2x4

3/8" CEDAR
PLYWOOD

Construct the Railing

Local building ordinances vary, but plan on making your railings at least 48 inches high with balusters that are no more than 1-3/4 inches apart. Remember to have this or any other railing design approved by your local building inspector.

Railing Considerations

Adapt the railing design shown here to accommodate your own deck's needs. For further explanation of the steps in rail construction, see "Deck Builder's Companion" (pages 20–21) and "Backyard Island" (pages 58–60).

When it comes to rail design, the key factors that come into play are your imagination and your budget.

▶ The railing design shown here is certainly worth the effort, but it did take two people a full five days to build.

▶ Use a combination predrilling and countersinking bit to speed inserting the many screws required.

▶ Stain all of the many railing parts before you install them.

▶ Cover the screw holes with a caulk that matches the color of the stain, or you can stain the caulk later.

Building the Railing

Follow the principles in the Railing Design Detail at left, adapting the specifics to your own design.

▶ Assemble the railing by cutting, plumbing, and screwing on the posts first.

▶ Next, screw on the top rails.

▶ Preassemble the baluster sections and screw them on (Photo 11).

2x4 TOP RAIL

2x2

TWO
SCREWS

PREASSEMBLED
SECTION

Photo 11. Assemble the railing by cutting, plumbing, and screwing on the railing posts first, then attaching the top rails. Preassemble the baluster sections, then screw them to the railing.

Construct the Gate and Pergola

The final steps are to add a secure gate and, if you choose, an arbor or pergola to shade the rectangular portion of the deck.

Gate Considerations

▶ It's easiest to build a gate on the ground, then hang the assembled unit. Adapt the specifications in the Construction Plan and Gate Detail on page 64 to your own needs.

▶ Allow 3 feet of width for one person to walk through and 4 feet for two together. The 42-inch width suggested in the Gate Detail is a happy medium.

▶ Two hinges are usually enough for a gate up to 4 feet high, but three are best for a taller one (see the Gate Detail).

Building the Gate

▶ Find the locations you marked earlier for the 4x6 gate posts. Dig the holes to 6 inches below the frost line, then set these posts in concrete, for greater stability.

▶ Assemble the unit, then mount the hinges—on the downhill side. Mask the hinges temporarily with plastic, then paint them and cut away the plastic (Photo 12).

▶ Install the latch and gate-closing device after the gate is hung. Make sure the closing device meets local building-code standards.

Building the Pergola

The pergola or arbor should now be added, if you decided to do so. Follow the suggested specifications in the Construction Plan and Pergola Detail on page 64. For further information, see the "Patio with a Sunscreen Pergola" project (pages 112–115).

▶ Add a freestanding post the same height as the three extra-long railing posts you erected earlier (see page 66).

▶ Prepare the crosspieces, perhaps scalloping their ends for a more finished look (see page 114).

▶ Bolt the pieces together with 3/8-inch carriage bolts (Photo 13).

▶ Screw the cedar 2x2 shading pieces to these crosspieces at 2-inch intervals. Optionally, add sunscreen cloth at this stage (see page 115).

With the addition of the pergola you have completed a dramatic enhancement to your pool area. The next item of business? Invite over all your helpers for a pool party.

CONSTRUCT THE GATE AND PERGOLA

Photo 12. Support the gate with removable blocks. Add a gate latch and an automatic closing device that meets local building codes. Mask the hinges with plastic, then cut it away after painting the hinges.

Photo 13. Construct the pergola using extra-long railing posts for three corners. Add a fourth, free-standing, post that height. Assemble the frame using 3/8-in. carriage bolts. Screw cedar 2x2s to the top.

Lighting a Deck
or Patio

On those delicious summer evenings when the weather is ideal and everyone

is having a really terrific time, it would be a shame to have to leave your deck

or patio just because the sun is setting.

You can make such an evening last as long as you like simply by installing a

low-voltage lighting system like one of those shown here.

Adding low-voltage lighting will enhance the appearance of your porch or deck and make it much safer, too.

Before You Start

All you need to install your own deck or patio lighting is a weatherproof 120-volt outlet, the most basic hand tools, and a few hours of spare time. Best of all, these low-voltage systems don't require taking the precautions necessary with household 120-volt systems, because they aren't powerful enough to give you a serious shock.

Plan Your Lighting System

For the greatest safety and best appearance, the first places you should install deck lights are at steps and handrails (Photo 1). Every deck design is different, of course, but in general try to locate lights so that they cast maximum illumination onto the stair treads.

The step lights on this deck were installed in the middle of the risers. Depending on the design of your own deck, you might also be able to install lights under the front lips of the stair treads or at the edges of stairs.

Railing lights should help you find the railing in the dark—but not interfere with using it. Here, lights were mounted on the posts at the top and bottom of the steps.

The top post light clearly identifies where the handrail begins, and the bottom light illuminates the path that leads to the deck. Path illumination like this is perhaps even more useful with patios.

When planning lighting to go around seating areas, keep the fixtures relatively low. The bench lights on this deck were placed at approximately the same height as the bench seat, so that they provide adequate light but don't shine in anyone's eyes (Photo 2). Because you want bench lighting to be comfortable and inviting, don't install lights on top of railings or posts, where they might shine in people's eyes and pose a safety hazard.

Photo 1. Be sure that your step lights will provide plenty of light to the treads. Mount handrail lights so they don't interfere with the use of the handrail.

Photo 2. Keep bench lights low enough so that they won't shine in people's eyes. Mounting them at the seat's height works well.

Select Your Lighting System

When shopping for a lighting system for your deck or patio, first select the appropriate components to compliment your particular setting, then calculate what transformer to use with the system you choose. While you are selecting the appropriate system for your setting, also consider whether you'll want additional components to accent features such as shrubs and trees.

Choosing Components

Most brands of deck lighting come with instructions that will help you make your choices of both lighting components and transformers. The components of 12-volt lighting systems are simple to connect, even for do-it-yourselfers who are novices at electrical work (Photo 3). If your kit doesn't include an exterior-type on-off switch, you'll want to add one to your shopping list.

As with standard light fixtures, low-voltage lighting systems come in many quality levels and prices. The lights shown here are top-of-the-line architectural grade fixtures featuring metal housings with a baked-on finish designed for years of use. Systems that have plastic housings are available at considerably lower cost.

You'll find low-voltage lighting components at most home centers, lawn and garden stores, full-service hardware stores, and lighting centers. You can buy individual lights and components or select complete kits that include all the necessary fixtures, wire, and transformers. While you're at it, lay in a supply of insulated electrical staples.

Selecting a Transformer

The heart of all low-voltage lighting systems is the transformer. To determine the size you'll need, add up the individual wattages of all the lights you plan to install. (If you think you might add more lights to your system at a later date, take them into account now, too.) The transformer you decide to use must have a wattage rating equal to or greater than that number. If you're planning to install a lot of lights on your deck or patio, or if you'll be adding lights to trees and shrubs later, you may need more than one transformer.

There are three types of low-voltage transformers to choose from.

▶ Manually operated transformers that require you to turn the lights on and off by hand.

▶ Automatic-timer transformers that let you preset their on and off times.

▶ Photocell-eye transformers, with or without a timer, that automatically turn the lights on at dusk and off at dawn (or whenever you choose, if they are equipped with a timer).

Most timer and photocell transformers incorporate a manual override switch. Again, their price will be commensurate with their wattage rating and features.

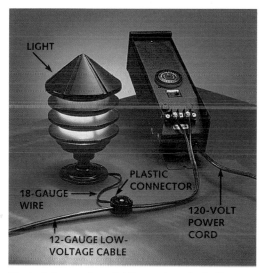

LIGHT

PLASTIC CONNECTOR

18-GAUGE WIRE

120-VOLT POWER CORD

12-GAUGE LOW-VOLTAGE CABLE

Photo 3. Low-voltage lighting systems typically include a transformer, 12-gauge low-voltage power cable, plastic connectors, 18-gauge fixture wire, and the fixtures.

Install Your Lighting System

Locate the outlet you want to use, then determine if it has weatherproof ground-fault-circuit-interrupter (GFCI) protection, which is required nationwide for outdoor outlets, to prevent shocks. GFCI coverage is provided either by special circuit breakers in the service panel or through special receptacles. GFCI protection is identifiable by small reset buttons in the receptacles.

Connect the Transformer

Once you have made sure the outlet you are going to use is protected, attach the transformer with screws to the outside of the house near the 120-volt outlet. Don't worry if there is no outlet directly on or adjacent to your deck or patio. Most transformers come with at least 6 feet of power cord to give you some flexibility in placement. If you don't have an outlet within range of the cord, you'll have to install one; don't use an extension cord, even a heavy-duty one. If you're inexperienced with high-voltage electrical work, hire a licensed electrician for this part of the job. Some codes in fact require a licensed electrician to do this. If you feel confident that you can do this job safely, proceed cautiously, but only after you have checked that the power really is turned off (see box on facing page).

Lay the Cable

Laying out low-voltage cable is easy. Starting at the transformer, run a continuous length of cable that reaches every location where you'll be installing a light. Allow about 12 inches of slack between individual lights so you'll be able to adjust their final positions.

For cable that runs along or under the deck or patio frame itself, use insulated electrical staples to attach wires to the wood framing. For cable runs along the ground, you can either camouflage the wires with mulch or bury them.

Attach the Fixtures

All that remains to be done now is to wire up the lighting fixtures and then mount them exactly where you want them on your deck or patio.

▶ Connect the transformer, cable, and lights according to the steps in Photos 4–7 (right).

▶ Following the installation instructions supplied with your kit, attach each fixture's base.

Finally, after you have installed the bulbs and tested them, you are ready to throw the switch and enjoy your evening.

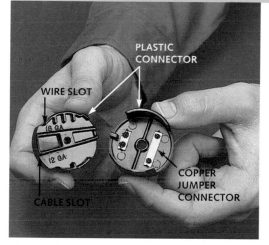

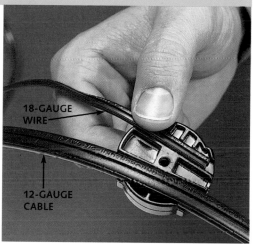

Photo 4. Separate the two sections of the plastic connector. Slots for cable and wire are marked with their gauge number and sized to fit. The copper jumpers connect the cable and wire.

Photo 5. Lay the wires or cables into their designated slots. Don't worry if they aren't completely flat. The other half of the connector will hold them in place once the two sections are screwed together.

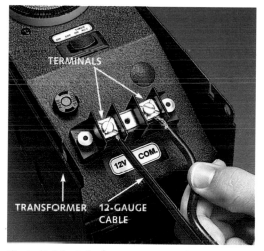

Photo 6. Screw the two pieces of the connector together. Make a sandwich out of the two connector pieces, then squeeze them together over the cable and wire before driving in the screw.

Photo 7. Attach the bare copper wires from the low-voltage cable to the transformer terminals. Don't worry about which wire attaches to which terminal. You don't have to maintain polarity.

SAFETY TECHNIQUE
Is the Power Really Off?

Before you begin working with electrical wiring, make sure the power is turned off. To test a receptacle, insert the leads of a circuit tester into the slots where the plug goes. The circuit is on if the tester's bulb lights. If it does not, this may mean only that the tester's leads were too short or too thick to go in far enough for good electrical contact; it does not mean that the power is off.

Check further by removing the receptacle's faceplate screws and mounting ears at the top and bottom, gripping the ears, and pulling the fixture straight out, being careful not to let its terminal screws touch metal. Now touch one lead of the tester to a brass screw terminal where a red- or black-insulated wire is connected, the other to a silver screw having a white-insulated wire. If the circuit is off, the tester's bulb will not light. Check also between the brass/black (or red)-wire terminal and the terminal where the bare or green-insulated grounded wire is connected, and between the silver/white-insulated wire terminal and the grounding-wire terminal. If the tester's light glows in either case, the power is still on.

Deck First Aid

Decks lead a hard life—and they start to show it all too quickly.

After ten years or so of exposure to sun, rain, and snow, a deck may exhibit

steps that are cracked and rotting away, railings that have warped

or become unsafe and ugly, deck boards with dozens of popped nailheads or cracks,

and joists and support posts showing signs of rot.

Unless your deck is brand-new, it probably has at least some of these problems.

The do-it-yourself first-aid treatments here require only a modest amount of skill, money,

and tools, and they can make your old deck look like new.

A deck that's seen better days not only detracts from the appearance of your home but may also have become unsafe to use. A few easy first-aid fixes can remedy its ailments.

Some of the most common symptoms of an aging deck are those seen here.

Nail pops

Cracks

Gaps

Rotted steps

Warped railings

Preliminaries

The first thing to do is to determine how much work you have ahead of you. You may be looking at nothing more than a power washing, followed by setting some popped nails and applying fresh stain or sealer. Or you may find that a major renovation is called for.

Power Washing

Giving your deck a good power washing should be your first move (Photo 1). Until you peel off the layers of grime covering the wood you won't really be able to gauge how much work you face. At first you may think that all the deck boards are beyond salvaging, but after washing them you might find that most are actually in pretty good shape. With luck you might discover that you need to replace only part of the decking.

To make the most of the power washing, first scrub into the deck a deck cleaner recommended for your type of wood. Then rinse it off with the power washer. You'll not only remove layers of built-up dirt but also expose fresh wood fibers, which will make the surface look new. Once you're done with the deck, you may want to clean the patio, driveway, or sidewalks while you have the washer.

Setting Popped Nails

After you have treated your deck to a power washing, you'll appreciate how much better it looks, but you may also notice that it has more popped nails than it did before. Power washing not only removes years of built-up dirt and grime but also dislodges surface wood fibers in the process.

Resetting popped nails with a nail set is only the first step of the repair. If that were all you did, the nails would soon work their way back up, because there's not enough wood left in the original nail holes to provide good purchase for them. In addition to resetting all the popped nails, do the following.

▶ Drive each nail below the surface of the wood with a nail set, to avoid dimpling the surface of the wood (Photo 2).

▶ Predrill a pilot hole, then drive a galvanized deck screw alongside the nail so that the screw head overlaps part of the nailhead to hold it down (Photo 3).

Estimating Time and Cost

Power washing the deck and resetting popped nails will take about half a day each. Expenses will include renting a 1,000-psi washer and purchasing deck cleaner and galvanized deck screws.

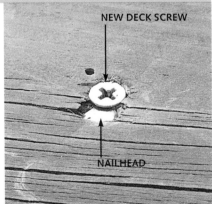

Photo 1. Clean the deck thoroughly with a 1,000-psi power washer. This single step may reveal that the deck is in better shape than you thought.

Photo 2. Setting popped nails is a two-step process. To avoid dimpling, first use a nail set to drive the nailhead back down below the surface of the wood.

Photo 3. After you have set the popped nail, drive a deck screw alongside it so that the head of the screw covers the nailhead, locking the nail in place.

Analyze the Job

Once you have power washed the deck and reset all the popped nails, give your deck a careful inspection, writing down everything that needs attention. Note damaged deck boards and steps, rotted wood that looks water damaged and lets you easily insert a jackknife blade, and dangerous steps or railings. And, of course, jot down any cosmetic surface treatments that your deck will need to look its best again.

Estimating Time and Cost

With your repair list in hand, calculate the cost in time and money for these repairs. Use the following checklist as a guide.

▶ **Stain or paint the deck.** You will need stain or paint and other supplies and about two days time total.

▶ **Replace stair stringers and treads.** Buy pressure-treated 2x12's and 2x6's. Estimate one to two days to finish.

▶ **Rout new edges on old deck boards.** You'll have to buy or rent a router and perhaps buy a round-over bit. This will take one to two days to complete.

▶ **Replace deck boards.** Estimate the number of boards. And for the lumber-intensive jobs like this one you may find it worthwhile renting a power miter box. This work may require a few hours to one day.

▶ **Replace a pressure-treated support post.** It will take a few hours for an above-ground replacement, more if posts are on in-ground footings and/or the tops of the posts do double duty as deck railing posts.

▶ **Replace a deck joist.** You'll need joists and metal joist hangers. This will take a few hours to a half day, depending on the ease of access you enjoy.

▶ **Build a new railing.** See the Stair and Railing Detail on page 88. Estimate costs by the 4-foot section, and assume it will take three hours for each such section.

▶ **Build light towers.** See Photo 21 on page 89. This will depend on the light fixture chosen and take half a day to build; the wiring time will vary.

▶ **Add low-voltage lights to the deck's steps.** See Photo 22 on page 89. Allow a half day.

Now schedule a visit with your local building inspector. First determine together whether there's major structural damage or merely a need for general repair. If posts, beams, or stairs need replacement, check with the local building-code office. You might choose not to consult them, however, if you find that less than half the decking or railings requires replacement.

Skills, Tools, and Materials

Deck repair requires only basic carpentry skills, and because all deck components are exposed to view it's easy to figure out how they come apart and how they need to go back together again.

You'll need just the basic power tools: a circular saw, a router, an electric drill that can double as a screwdriver, and, if you have a lot of lumber to replace, a power miter saw. Power miter boxes, as well as routers, also are available at rental centers. The basic hand tools you'll need are a hammer, a framing square, an adjustable square, a small sledgehammer, a 3-foot level, and a measuring tape.

All new wood should be either pressure-treated or a rot-resistant species such as redwood, cedar, or cypress. You'll probably want to match the original wood type that was used when the deck was built.

Use only exterior-type finish: semitransparent stain for areas that receive foot traffic, solid color stain for no traffic areas. Check the product label to make sure you're using the right finish.

Tools You Need

Hand Tools

Adjustable square

Framing square

Hammer

Measuring tape

Nail set

Small sledgehammer

3-ft. level

Power Tools

Circular saw

Drill

Router

Miter saw

Miter box (rented)

Pressure washer (rented)

Repair Deck Stairs

Because stairs probably get the heaviest use of any part of your deck, they are the most likely candidates for some repair work. First check your deck's stair treads for cracks and signs of rot. Then check the stair stringers—the big sawtooth sections of lumber that support the treads on each end and the middle. In case both are damaged, the discussion that follows will show you how to replace everything. You'll probably need to remove sections of your deck railing to complete this job. If the railing is in good condition and you'll be reinstalling it later, take special care in removing it.

▶ Unscrew or unbolt the old set of stairs, or, if this proves unworkable, cut through its fasteners with a reciprocating saw or hacksaw. With assistance from a helper, remove the old stairs (Photo 4).

▶ Use one of the old stair stringers as a template to lay out the new stringers on 2x12's (Photo 5). Then cut the stringers with a circular saw and complete the job by using a handsaw at each corner (Photo 6).

▶ There are two main ways to attach the stringers to the deck rim joist. Either the stringers will attach to the outside of the rim joist (Photo 7) or their last notch will tuck under the rim joist. If the stringers do tuck under, make sure that those notch portions are large enough to let you secure them fully to the rim joist.

▶ Attach the new stairs, using the same method as for the old ones, provided that method meets with the building inspector's approval. In Photo 7 the stringers were screwed to the rim joists with 4-inch galvanized deck screws.

▶ Rebuild the stairs, with or without 1x8 risers, the vertical pieces of wood above the stair treads (Photo 8). Risers will add to the cost in both time and money, but they will give your deck added strength and a more finished look. Attach the risers using a drill and screwdriver bit and 2-inch galvanized deck screws.

▶ Finally, install new 2x6 stair treads from "bullnose" treated lumber—boards with rounded edges—or whatever wood your deck requires. Fasten the treads with 3-1/2 inch galvanized deck screws.

If you're not immediately reinstalling the old railing, rig up a temporary one of 2x4's and bright-colored rope so no one accidentally walks off the deck's edge.

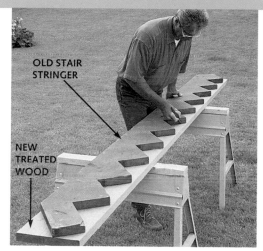

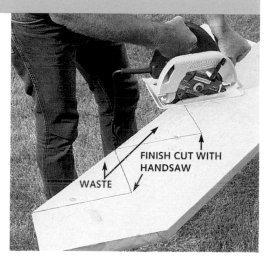

Photo 4. Removing rotted-out stairs requires help. Detach the whole unit at once, by unscrewing or unbolting it or cutting its fasteners.

Photo 5. Mark the dimensions for the new 2x12 stair stringers, by simply laying the old stringer on top of them to use as a template.

Photo 6. Cut out the new stair stringer with a circular saw, following the lines drawn in the last step. Finish the cut with a handsaw.

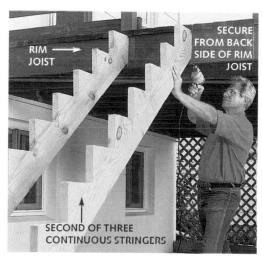

Photo 7. Screw the new stringers to the rim joist with 4-in. galvanized screws. If your stairs were attached differently, reinstall them the same way.

Photo 8. Use a drill with a screwdriver bit and deck screws to install new 2x6 treads. Leave a 1/8-in. gap between each pair of 2x6's, using 16d nails as spacers.

Replace Defective Joists and Posts

If inspection reveals that all of your joists have rotted, you'll need to remove and replace each one. But if only a few are damaged, you can save yourself a lot of time and work by leaving each old joist in place and installing a new one alongside it.

▶ Wood rot is contagious, so don't attach new joists directly to old, rotted ones. When installing a new joist beside an old one, be sure to allow some space between them. Install them 3 to 4 inches apart, being careful to leave just enough room so that you can swing a hammer.

▶ From treated lumber, cut the new joist to size. Use galvanized nails to attach new metal joist hangers (Photo 9).

▶ With a helper, lift the joist into position and nail it in place. Wait until you've replaced any damaged deck boards to attach the decking to the new joists. Use two galvanized deck screws or nails for each new joist.

▶ Before replacing a rotted deck post, first provide additional support for the deck. One way to do this is to build a temporary post from 2x4's and then wedge it tightly into place (Photo 10). If you're unable simply to unbolt the old post and slide it out, cut it in half with a handsaw.

▶ Cut a new 4x4 treated-wood post to length, put it in position, and drill holes for new zinc-plated carriage bolts. Drive the bolts home with a hammer (Photo 11), install new washers and nuts, and, finally, remove the temporary support.

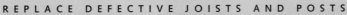

REPLACE DEFECTIVE JOISTS AND POSTS

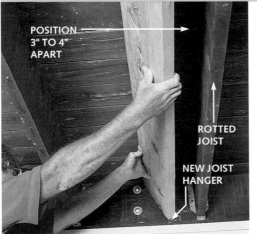

Photo 9. Install a new treated-wood joist and joist hanger parallel to but far enough away from any joist that's showing signs of rot so there's room to hammer.

Photo 10. Unbolt and remove a rotted post. First wedge in place a temporary support built from 2x4's. If necessary, cut out the old post with a handsaw.

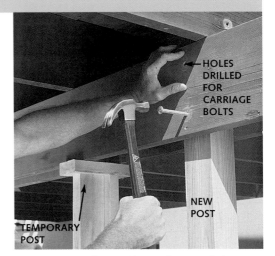

Photo 11. Pound new galvanized carriage bolts through pilot holes drilled in the new post. Avoid reusing any of the old fasteners.

Substitute New Deck Boards for Damaged Ones

If you're lucky, the earlier power washing revealed that the surfaces of your deck boards weren't as damaged as you thought. For confirmation, inspect the boards from below, testing with a jackknife.

If the undersides of some boards appear to be in good condition, don't replace them. Instead, remove all of the decking and proceed as follows to reuse the old pieces most economically.

▶ Discard any severely damaged boards. You can reuse most of the decking, however, by flipping it over. Rout bullnose edges on the opposite sides. Then reinstall the flipped-over decking pieces—in their original locations. When the deck was first laid, its convex, bark side should have faced up, because this is the tougher surface. But even though you'll now lay these boards with their soft sides facing up, this strategy still makes sense on an older deck, to help you get your money's worth out of the material.

▶ If you have easy access from below, pound the deck boards up with a small sledgehammer and a block of scrap wood (Photo 12). If you don't have access from underneath the deck, pry up or cut away some of the boards. Remove one or two boards at a time and rout new edges on their opposite sides (Photo 13). Be absolutely sure no nails or screws remain in the wood before you begin routing.

▶ Install the flipped-over deck boards and any new pieces with galvanized deck screws (Photo 14). As much as possible, reuse the old nail holes on the recycled deck boards, reinstalling each board after you work on it. That way you won't need to cut anything except the new boards.

SUBSTITUTE NEW DECK BOARDS FOR DAMAGED ONES

SMALL SLEDGEHAMMER

SCRAP WOOD BLOCK

Photo 12. Remove deck boards without damaging them by pounding from underneath, if you have access. Use a small sledge and a wood block.

NEW ROUTED EDGE

Photo 13. Flipping over old deck boards and reusing them will reduce your materials costs. Rout a bullnose edge on the deck boards you're going to reuse.

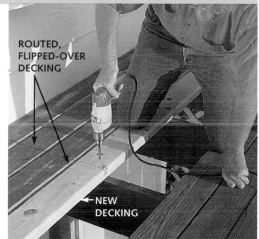

ROUTED, FLIPPED-OVER DECKING

NEW DECKING

Photo 14. Secure flipped-over deck boards and any new decking with galvanized deck screws. On reused boards, drive new screws through old nail holes.

New Deck Railing

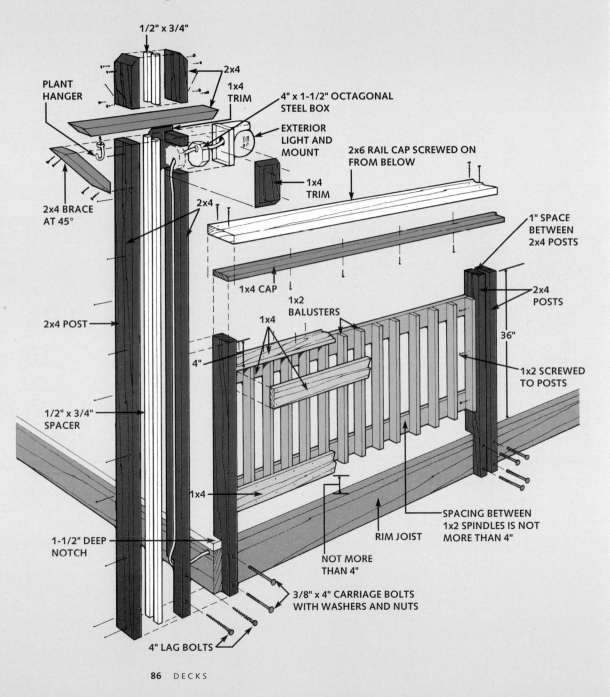

1/2" x 3/4"

2x4

1x4 TRIM

PLANT HANGER

4" x 1-1/2" OCTAGONAL STEEL BOX

EXTERIOR LIGHT AND MOUNT

2x6 RAIL CAP SCREWED ON FROM BELOW

1x4 TRIM

2x4 BRACE AT 45°

2x4

1" SPACE BETWEEN 2x4 POSTS

2x4 POST

1x4 CAP

1x2 BALUSTERS

1x4

2x4 POSTS

36"

4"

1x2 SCREWED TO POSTS

1/2" x 3/4" SPACER

1-1/2" DEEP NOTCH

1x4

RIM JOIST

SPACING BETWEEN 1x2 SPINDLES IS NOT MORE THAN 4"

NOT MORE THAN 4"

3/8" x 4" CARRIAGE BOLTS WITH WASHERS AND NUTS

4" LAG BOLTS

Build a New Deck Railing

Constructing a new deck railing may be the biggest part of your whole renovation. Not only does the railing need to look good, it also has to comply with current building codes, which generally limit openings between balusters to no wider than 4 inches.

This is a good time to look ahead and decide whether or not to add light towers (see page 89) before proceeding with building new deck railings.

▶ The first step is to plan a railing design that complements your deck (see the detail at left). Make sure to have your plans and materials approved by the local building inspector. Then you can demolish the old railing (Photo 15). To prevent people from absentmindedly walking off the edge of the deck, put up a temporary safety barrier of 2x4's and colored nylon rope.

▶ First cut all parts to length so you start out with a big "kit" of railing components. A power miter box will save you time here. Because you'll be duplicating many pieces, clamp the boards together and transfer their measurements to several pieces at once for speed and accuracy (Photo 16).

▶ Once all the pieces have been cut, find a level spot on which to work (or use the deck) and begin building the railing sections.

Four-foot modules work well in most situations, but you may want to use another size if it fits your decks better. Nail together the 1x4's and 1x2's with 4d galvanized nails (Photo 17). On each section, leave a space for the 1x2 rails at the ends. Later you'll attach these pieces directly to the posts.

▶ Trim the 2x4 posts to length, then cut the lower notch to fit over the deck rim joist as in the plan at left. Drill pilot holes for the zinc-plated carriage bolts, then drive the bolts with a hammer (Photo 18). Position the paired 2x4's with 1 inch of space between them. Then center the railing-end 1x2's on the inside faces of the posts and screw them in place.

▶ Now, with a helper, lower each assembled section of railing into place between the 2x4 posts. Align the sections using the 1x2's you just attached to the 2x4 posts (Photo 19).

▶ Finally, measure and cut the 1x4 base caps and 2x6 rail caps to span several sections of railing on each side of the deck. Attach the base cap first, then secure the rail caps by driving deck screws through the 1x4 base caps from below (see the detail at left and Photo 20).

Photo 15. Remove the old railing using a pry bar, hammer, or saw. For safety, install a temporary railing made from 2x4's and bright-colored nylon rope.

Photo 16. Clamp the material for the railing together and transfer all dimensions to the pieces at once. This speeds the work and also reduces the possibility of error.

Photo 17. Assemble the new railing on a level surface, building it in 4-ft. segments or whatever increments work best for the type and dimensions of your deck.

Photo 18. Bolt the 2x4 posts in place. Drive the bolts through pilot holes after cutting them to length, notching them so they fit the deck's rim joist.

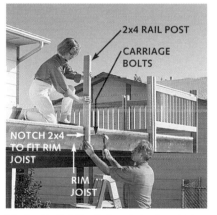

Photo 19. Slide a section of railing into place between two sets of posts. A 1x2 screwed to the corner of each 2x4 will make it easier to position the railing.

Photo 20. Screw the 2x6 rail cap into place from below the 1x4 rail top. Cut the 1x4 base cap and 2x6 rail cap long enough to cover several sections of railing.

Stair and Railing

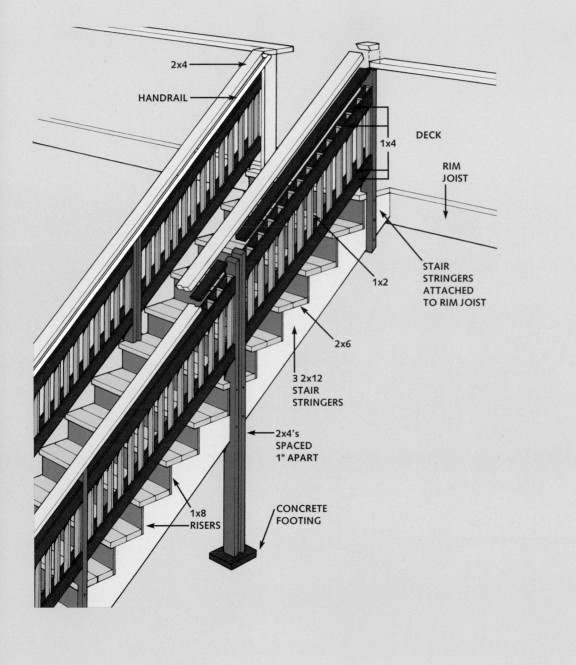

2x4

HANDRAIL

1x4

DECK

RIM
JOIST

STAIR
STRINGERS
ATTACHED
TO RIM JOIST

1x2

2x6

3 2x12
STAIR
STRINGERS

2x4's
SPACED
1" APART

1x8
RISERS

CONCRETE
FOOTING

Build a New Stair Railing

Make a new stair railing by using the same dimensions and design as the deck railing. The only difference is the adjustment you'll need to make for the angle of the staircase (see the Stair and Railing Detail, left).

▶ Notch the 2x4 posts to fit the stair treads, then bolt them in place. For a long staircase, extend the center pair of 2x4 posts to ground level and attach them to concrete footings. For more information on footings, see Build a Solid Foundation on pages 16–17.

▶ When the posts are in place, measure the angle necessary for cutting the 1x4 side and top pieces of the railing sections. Then nail each section's 1x2's between the 1x4 side pieces so they're perpendicular to the stair treads. As before, don't attach the end 1x2's to the individual stair-rail sections. Instead, center and secure them to the inside faces of the 2x4 posts to help position the railing sections after you slide them into position.

▶ Install the 2x4 rail cap. Although the deck railing uses a 2x6 instead of a 2x4 and a 1x4 base cap, the stair rail uses a single 2x4 cap, because most building codes require a narrower rail that is easy to grasp. Many localities will require you to install a standard handrail, as done for this project, to meet safety requirements. Check with your building inspector for details on this and the fastening hardware required.

Light Your Deck

If you decide to include light towers in your deck upgrade, build the towers before you install the deck railings.

▶ Build the towers from 2x4's with 1/2-inch spacers cut from either a 1x4 or a 1x6 (see the New Deck Railing Detail on page 86).

▶ Run the electrical line up the hollow center of each tower to a metal electrical box. Use nonmetallic cable labeled UF (in Canada, NMWU), for outdoor or under-ground applications. Then install the exterior light fixture of your choice. Two 1x4 trim pieces screwed to the vertical 2x4s will hide the rest of the box.

▶ These light towers were designed to fit flush against the deck railings (Photo 21). Position them at the deck corners, then drill pilot holes for 4 inch lag bolts. Drive deck screws through the railing into the light towers, keeping the screws well away from the electrical line.

▶ Add low-voltage deck lights to the steps (Photo 22). Simply screw the light housings in place and then run the power cords to a transformer plugged into an outdoor-type ground-fault circuit-interrupt (GFCI) outlet.

Finishing Touches

Because your deck renovation will probably leave you with bright new wood intermingled with older pieces, you'll want to try for a uniform finish with new stain. Deck stains now come in a wide assortment of colors. You might want to consider staining your revitalized deck with several colors, rather than taking the conventional approach of staining it all one color.

Use semitransparent deck stain on areas that get foot traffic and solid-color stain everywhere else. Each gallon of stain typically covers 200 to 400 square feet of surface area, depending on the wood's porosity. So if you use 300 square feet as an average, you can estimate how much stain you'll need. Some brands are available in economical 5-gallon cans.

The easiest way to apply stain to deck boards is with a paint roller on an extension handle. Allow 48 hours' drying time.

Safety Tip

Don't "economize" by sawing short pieces of scrap wood into still-shorter pieces. The price could be serious injury from kickback. Don't use a power saw on any piece that's too short to clamp or hold securely. Most pros won't use a piece less than 2 ft. long.

LIGHT YOUR DECK

FLUSH WITH 2x4 RAIL POSTS ON BOTH SIDES

USE 4" LAG SCREWS

Photo 21. Assemble each light tower on the ground first. Then, with help, drill the mounting holes and attach it to the rim joist with 4-in. lag bolts.

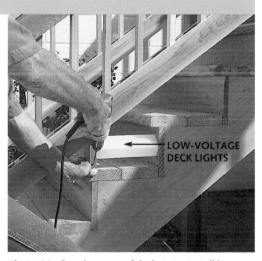

LOW-VOLTAGE DECK LIGHTS

Photo 22. On a long run of deck stairs, install low-voltage deck lights. They're inexpensive and easy to install, and simply plug into an outdoor GFCI outlet.

Patios

Patio and Pathway

A nicely designed paver patio makes an attractive, practical addition to any

backyard. And a durable, easy-to-install paver pathway is a good way to link your new

patio with the driveway, house, or deck.

The projects shown here are basic, but you can customize them to suit your home

and grounds. The reward for your efforts will be a comfortable place to play,

barbecue, garden, or simply relax in your yard.

The paver patio being built at the left will turn an underused backyard area into an attractive outdoor room. And the paver pathway above would be inviting whatever its destination.

Lay a Paver Patio

Tools You Need

Hand Tools

Carpenter's level

Hand tamper (home-made)

Mallet, wood block

Mason's chisel

Measuring tapes (2)

Safety goggles, dust mask

Stakes and string (mason's cord)

Optional

Mechanical vibrator plate (rented)

Tub saw with diamond blade (rented)

Paving stones come in a wide variety of shapes and sizes—either natural or factory-made. Some are bricks that have been baked especially hard to withstand years of wear and tear. Others are made from concrete. They are formed in many shapes, colors, and textures to suit many different designs.

The general procedures used in this project are the ones you'd use to create any paver patio. So read through this section carefully and then plug in your own design elements.

Before You Begin

The patio shown here is a large one—12 feet by 16 feet. It is a big project that requires some experience in leveling surfaces and making square corners. It also involves a good deal of digging and shoveling, which are the most labor-intensive parts of the project. The process of setting the patio stones is a much easier job, however, one even the children can help with. Allow several weekends to complete a patio of this size—one for laying it out and completing the excavation work, and the others for setting the stones. You'll need only basic hand tools and optional power tools, which can be rented at home centers.

Plan Your Paver Patio

A well-designed patio must take into account the terrain, landscape, and the needs and pocketbook of your family. Not all yards are candidates for a patio. In uneven terrain, a raised deck—which can span hill and dale—might be the best option for outdoor space.

You may want your patio to tie in with existing trees, planting beds, decks, borders, and privacy screens. Whatever your plans, first measure everything and make a small scale drawing of your home and existing landscape. You can use a straight, 16-ft. 2x4 with a 4-ft. level on it and a tape measure to get a rough idea of how much your yard slopes (note that on your drawing, too). Then lay tracing paper on top of the scale drawing and doodle a few patio designs.

Here are some useful planning guidelines.
▶ Ask yourself how you'll be using your patio. One expert recommends a minimum length of at least 16 feet long in one direction as often being the most functional. Plan for at least a 6x6 foot area out of any traffic path for a dining table and chairs. Do you need space for a grill? Lounge chairs? A wading pool? Planters? Hopscotch? Sketch these on your tracing paper as you doodle.
▶ In small areas, use simple pavers and patterns (like the running bond shown on

page 97). In large areas, you can break up the expanse with a variety of patterns of dividing bands.
▶ Curves add interest and grace to the patio—but also loads of cutting and extra work.

Design Your Patio

A basic patio is relatively easy to design.
▶ First, simply lay out its approximate dimensions with stakes and string.
▶ Adjust the shape to allow for the custom features you included in your initial sketches. Now take a sketch of your plan (complete with the rough dimensions) to a landscaping specialist, who can help you select the right paving material that will turn your design concept into reality.
▶ Choose materials for the two main components of your patio: the actual patio stones and the materials that make up the border. Patio stones are available in a variety of shapes, colors, and sizes. Narrow your choices, then compare the price per square foot for each type of paver on your list. For border materials you can choose from treated lumber, plastic, stone, and metal. Aside from cost, your primary consideration in choosing a border material is whether it can be used as edging for your particular choice of paving material. Consult your dealer for advice.

Lay Out the Patio

First, use stakes and string to lay out a rectangle that approximates the shape of your patio. Your string line doesn't need to follow the perimeter outline on your plan exactly. You can incorporate minor variations later (see the Paver Patio Layout, right).

The 3–4–5 Method

To help lay the patio stones accurately, establish parallel and perpendicular sides on your rough layout using the 3–4–5 triangle method (see the diagram at right).

▶ Measure 3 feet along a straight base line, in this case the base of the house.

▶ With two measuring tapes and a helper, measure exactly 4 feet from one end of the 3-foot line and 5 feet from the other.

▶ Drive a stake at the exact point where the 4- and 5-foot marks meet. The angle of the corner opposite the 5-foot side of the triangle you have just created will be precisely 90 degrees (a right angle).

▶ With a string line, extend the 4-foot side of the triangle to establish the width of the patio. (For larger patios, you can increase your accuracy by doubling the original triangle's dimensions to 6, 8, and 10 feet.)

▶ Extend the 3-foot side to establish the length of the patio.

▶ Drive stakes now to mark the four corners of the patio.

Paver Patio Layout

After laying out your patio's approximate dimensions with stakes and string, establish a true 90-degree corner by using the 3–4–5 method explained in the text.

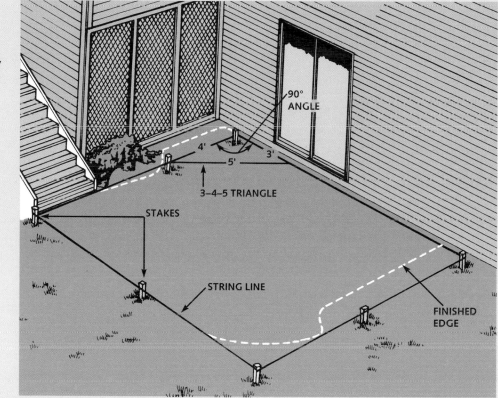

Create a Slope

Patios must have a slight slope (1 inch for every 4 to 8 feet) for proper drainage. If you don't provide enough slope, rainwater will settle into low spots, eventually softening and washing out the sand and subbase materials beneath. A flat or poorly sloped patio could even direct water into your basement. Too much slope and you'll feel you're on a listing ship. Bear in mind that you can build up low spots by applying an extra-thick layer of subbase.

▶ Set a level on a long, straight 2x4 and establish a level plane between the corner stakes (Photo 1). You can simplify this step by placing intermediate stakes every 6 to 8 feet. Later you can use these stakes as guides as you lay the stones.

▶ Mark the slope on the stakes at the low edge of the patio. About 1 inch of drop for every 8 feet of distance from the house makes a good, gradual slope.

▶ Indicate the proper slope on the intermediate stakes you have placed.

Now determine the height of your patio. This patio's surface was 8 inches below the first tread of a stairway (Photo 2). The patio height should also be level with, or perhaps even slightly higher than, the surrounding ground so that rainwater will drain off into the surrounding grass.

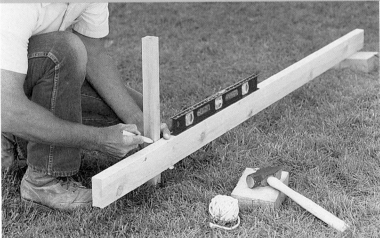 

CREATE A SLOPE

Photo 1. Mark a level line on the stakes at the perimeter of the patio. Establish a drainage slope of 1 in. for every 8 ft. from the house.

Photo 2. Establish the finished height. Then add up the thicknesses of the patio stones, the sand, and base and excavate to that depth.

Patio Building Materials

Patio and Pathway Detail

Once you have compacted the excavated area with a hand or mechanical tamper, evenly spread enough aggregate so that it will be at least three inches deep when compressed. Then, once the aggregate is compacted and the edging is in place, add enough sand for a 1-in. thickness once it has been screeded smooth.

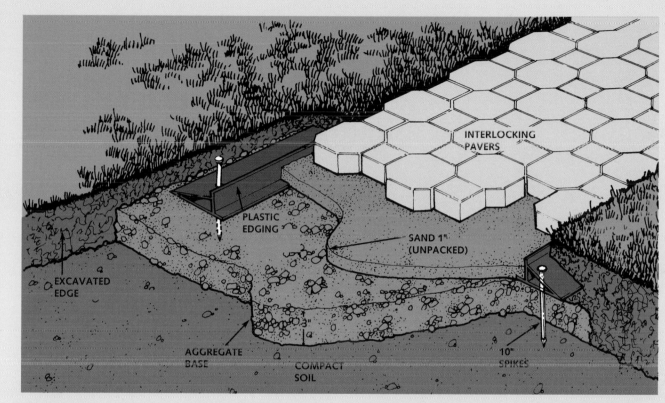

INTERLOCKING PAVERS

PLASTIC EDGING

SAND 1" (UNPACKED)

EXCAVATED EDGE

AGGREGATE BASE

3"

COMPACT SOIL

10" SPIKES

Paver Patterns

Simple rectangular pavers can be laid in a variety of patterns. Other paver shapes are available: squares, zigzags, keyholes, and even some that look like fancy floor tile. Shop around at home improvement and landscaping centers for more information.

Herringbone

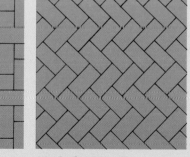

Herringbone at 45°

Running bond

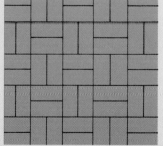

Basketweave

Shoveling Smart

A patio project almost always scores a 9.9 in sweat equity. You'll be amazed at the amount of dirt you remove, even with the smallest patio.

▶ Compacted earth, once dug up and tossed, tends to double its previous size. Move it as few times as possible—preferably just once. If you're going to use the dirt to fill in a low area, shovel the sod and dirt right into the wheelbarrow and dump it in its final resting spot. If it's going to be hauled away, back in the trailer, truck, or trash bin as close as you can.

▶ Be equally wise with the materials you haul in. Do all your excavating, then have your subbase dumped directly on the patio site. Have your leveling sand and pavers delivered close to the patio. A patio could take hundreds if not thousands of pavers—that's a lot of hauling by hand! Consider access to your backyard. Can you back a truck close to the patio site? If not, are you prepared to do a lot of hauling by wheelbarrow? Will a heavy truck damage any tree roots or your soft asphalt driveway on a hot day? Have you carefully figured the amount of materials you need before ordering, so you don't wind up with tons of extra sand, subbase or pavers? Does it make sense to temporarily remove a section of fence for access during the project?

▶ Finally, consider recruiting help for some of the more labor-intensive work: excavating, spreading the subbase, and lugging the pavers.

Build the Base

The better you prepare the base for the pavers, the more years you can expect from your new patio. How deep you need to dig will depend on your soil. If your soil is low lying and wet, you'll need to lay a thicker base than on higher, well-drained soil.

Soil Preparation

▶ First, excavate the footprint of the patio deeply enough to allow for the base of packed aggregate, sand, and patio stones (see the Patio and Pathway Detail on the previous page and Photo 3). Use the reference lines you previously marked on the stakes to slope the bed properly as you dig it.

The subgrade should be free of all such organic matter as sod, grass roots, and soft and mucky ground. Dig out all poor soil. If some spots are very hard and others very soft, break up these areas and disperse the soil to provide uniform support.

On the other hand, do not routinely remove the soil under your patio area and replace it with fill. If the soil is already reasonably uniform and free of vegetable matter, it is better left alone. Nature has already done your compacting for you. Most sandy soils merely need tamping on the top portion disturbed by your spade.

However, if you do find that fill is needed, common fill materials are sand, gravel, crushed stone, or blast-furnace slag. Sand usually is preferred, because you can level it more easily. You can also use leftover soil from high spots as long as it is similar to the rest of your subgrade.

Compact the soil evenly with a hand tamper or mechanical vibrator plate.

Renting a mechanical vibrator will save time and effort (Photo 4). Use this vibrator later to compact the aggregate and again to pack down the pavers. For very small patios, a hand tamper may be all you'll need (one is in the background of Photo 4). If you don't want to rent a hand tamper, you can make one by nailing two 12-inch squares of 3/4-inch plywood to the end of a 4x4.

▶ Spread enough crushed stone so that it will be about three inches deep when well compacted. The recommended base material may be different in your region. Your local patio-stone dealer can recommend a suitable base and help you determine how much material you'll need. Your supplier can also help assemble and deliver the washed concrete sand, edge restraints, and patio stones you'll need.

▶ Compact the aggregate. Extra effort spent making sure that the base is uniformly flat and correctly sloped will pay off handsomely later, because the final surface of the finished patio will conform exactly to the top of the base, showing every dip and rise.

▶ Nail down the edge restraints with 10-inch spikes, following your string lines accurately (Photo 5). Incorporate any perimeter variations for features such as planters and curves (Photo 6). You may be able to adjust some of the edges later to avoid having to cut the final row of pavers.

▶ Add the sand and screed it smooth in sections that are about 6 feet square. To maintain a uniform 1-inch thickness of sand, drag the screed across 1-inch high border strips or sections of iron pipe temporarily placed at the sides of the section (Photo 7).

Photo 3. Remove sod from the patio area and 6 in. outside the borders. Follow the finished patio shape around the perimeter.

Photo 4. Compact the soil and then an aggregate base perfectly flat with a vibrator plate. Use the marks on your stakes to achieve the proper slope.

Photo 5. Align and fasten the plastic retaining edge to the base with 10-in. spikes. You can also use wood, metal, or stone edging.

Photo 6. Cut kerfs in the plastic edging with a hacksaw to make a smooth curve. Cut out wedge-shaped sections to make a curve in the other direction.

Photo 7. Pour sand and smooth a section at a time with a board run across two 1-in. high strips of wood. Then remove the strips and fill the grooves with sand.

Lay the Pavers

Lay the pavers on each screeded section before smoothing the next one. The patio shown here uses interlocking concrete pavers, which are available in several other shapes and colors. Specially cast edge pieces help minimize the amount of cutting at the patio edges (Photo 8).

If you find that your patio stones aren't aligning correctly, stop work to find and correct the problem (Photo 9).

▶ Check the starting corner to make sure it's exactly 90 degrees. Adjust the edge restraints as necessary.

▶ Successively tap each new stone in the same direction with a hammer handle. Eliminating the gaps between stones may correct the problem (Photo 10).

Photo 8. Start laying pavers from the 90-degree corner, beginning with the special edge pieces. Tap down the pavers with a hammer handle to set them.

Photo 9. Lay several rows of pavers at a time across the width of the patio. If the pavers don't align correctly, stop and fix the problem right then.

Photo 10. Lay the interlocking pavers without leaving gaps. Nudge the pavers tightly together by tapping their edges with a hammer handle.

Cut and Set the Pavers

When you cut the final edge pieces, make simple crosscuts by cracking the pavers with a hammer and a wide mason's chisel.

▶ To make angled and curved cuts quickly and accurately, rent a tub saw with a diamond blade (Photo 12). Always wear safety goggles and a dust mask whenever you cut or saw stone.

▶ Finally, set the pavers firmly into the sand with the vibrator plate (Photo 13). Use a mallet and a wood block to set the pavers in hard-to-reach areas. Sweep sand into the surface cracks and use the vibrator plate a final time to help the sand settle. Then sweep in additional sand (Photo 14). The sand will settle further and wash down after a few rains, so keep a supply of it handy to refill the gaps.

Photo 11. Leave any cutting of the pavers for the final step, doing them all at once. Hold the pavers in place while you mark the cut line.

Photo 12. Rent a tub saw with a diamond blade to cut the curves and angles on pavers. Wear safety goggles and a dust mask when you cut or saw stone.

Photo 13. Compress the pavers into the sand with a vibrator plate. Use a hammer and a wood block to set pavers in hard-to-reach areas.

Photo 14. Sweep sand into the gaps between the pavers. Use the vibrator plate again to help settle the sand. Add more sand as necessary.

Lay a Paver Pathway

A pathway can be part of a larger project or a project in itself. A walkway made from pavers is an attractive way to link your driveway to your front door, existing deck to new patio, or back door to garden area.

Plan Your Paver Pathway

Here are a few tips to make laying a paver pathway easier.

▶ Keep the patterns simple; a paver border running parallel to the path with a simple staggered pattern within it is often the most attractive alternative.

▶ Tilt the path slightly for drainage. One-half inch across a 3-foot wide path is adequate.

▶ Take extra care to keep the edgings an equal distance apart; it will make screeding, cutting, and paver laying easier.

Lay Out the Pathway

For a curved pathway, begin by laying out the walk roughly, using two lengths of garden hose or rope. If you want a path with straight sides, drive stakes at the corners and stretch mason's cord or string between them.

Build the Base and Border

Now prepare the base for the pathway as explained on page 98 for the patio project. Refer also to the Patio and Pathway Detail on page 97 for information on how to spread aggregate (crushed stone) and sand to build your pathway's base.

Once you have excavated the pathway area, compacted the soil, spread and compacted the aggregate, and nailed down the flexible plastic edging restraints for the pathway, following the patio-building steps outlined earlier in this chapter, you are ready to prepare the sand base.

As described in building the patio base, try to maintain a uniform 1-inch thickness of sand, pulling the wooden screed across temporary edging strips 1 inch higher than the surface of the aggregate. This time, however, you want to incorporate a slight pitch of about 1/2 inch across a 3-foot pathway so that water will drain off the path readily (Photo 1).

If your pathway is long, screed only as much as sand as you can cover with pavers in one working session. Screeded sand left over is almost guaranteed to be ruffled by wind and rain or passersby.

Now install the border, spacing the pavers evenly the width of a carpenter's pencil (Photo 2). On curves, draw along the pencil to mark the overlapping part to be trimmed off once all the pavers that need to be cut are marked this way. Angle-cut every other border paver around the curve. Incidentally, using half-pavers to border tight circles cuts down on the size of the pie-shaped pieces between each paver.

Lay and Landscape the Pathway

Once the borders are down, lay the pavers, using mason's cord or string as a guideline (Photo 3). Wait until later to cut all at once the odd-shaped pieces that butt against the border. Follow the steps on pages 100–101 for laying and cutting pavers, setting them with a vibrator plate, and filling between them with sand.

Finally, after the pathway is completed, landscape along its edges with flowers, shrubs, and grass. The grass will help particularly, by rooting up through open spaces in the flexible plastic edging to anchor it in position (Photo 4).

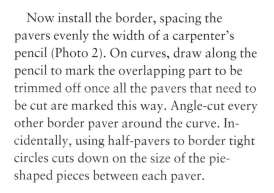

USE A PENCIL AS ANGLE GUIDE

NOTCHED SCREED BOARD

SLIGHT SIDE-TO-SIDE SLOPE

ANGLE-CUT EVERY OTHER BORDER PAVER AT CURVE

Photo 1. Smooth and level the sand, including a slight tilt of about 1/2 in. across a 3-ft. wide walkway.

Photo 2. Install the border, marking and cutting every other paver at an angle in curved areas.

LAYOUT STRING

SQUARES IN FLEXIBLE EDGING

Photo 3. Lay the pavers, using mason's cord or string as a guideline. Wait to cut and install the pieces that butt up to the border all at once.

Photo 4. Finally, landscape around the completed walkway and patio. Grass will root through the open spaces in the flexible edging to hold it in place.

Patio with a Sunscreen Pergola

Concrete, stone, and brick all suggest permanence. But it's not just

their toughness that makes brick pavers the natural choice for a patio.

They're also low-maintenance, dimensionally consistent units that

come in a variety of colors.

This paver patio is complemented by a sunscreen pergola that lets in just enough sun

so you can enjoy summer's warmth without having to face unwanted glare.

The simple design of the pergola shown at the right allows it to be freestanding or,

if you prefer, attached directly to your house.

Adding a brick patio is one of the easiest and most cost-effective ways to improve your yard. The crowning touch is a free-standing pergola with a sunscreen fabric that works with decorative stringers to shield the patio's occupants.

Patio Construction Plan

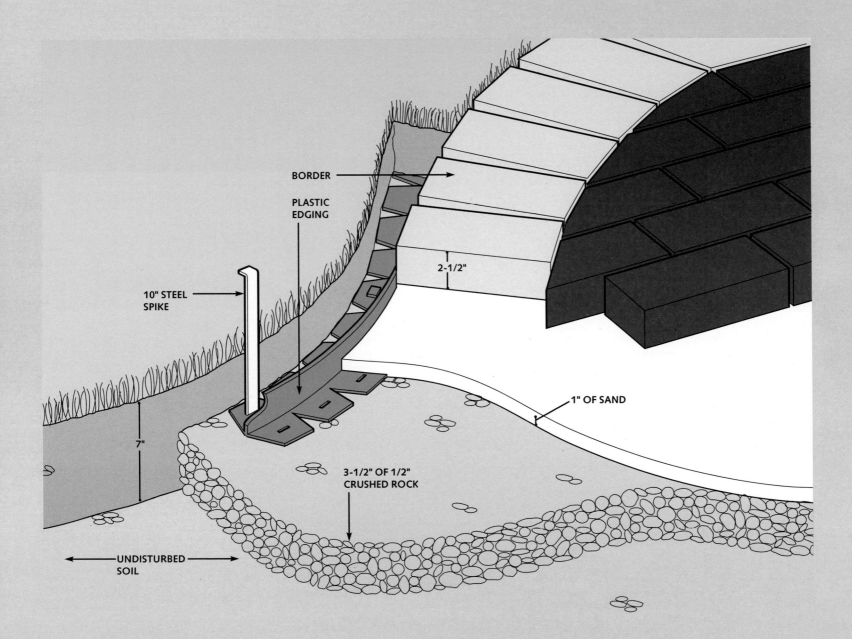

BORDER

PLASTIC
EDGING

2-1/2"

10" STEEL
SPIKE

1" OF SAND

7"

3-1/2" OF 1/2"
CRUSHED ROCK

UNDISTURBED
SOIL

The Paver Patio

Plan Your Paver Patio

Once you have your stone patio laid, it will last a long time. (Italy's two-thousand-year-old stone Appian Way is still in use today.) So place yours carefully, to make the best use of your site's slopes and sun angles.

Location and Budget

Choose a site that's fairly level, with a slope of no more than 2 inches per 10 feet of distance from the house. A slope this slight is barely noticeable, but will provide necessary drainage.

When budgeting for a patio project like this, consider more than just the cost of the pavers, crushed rock, and sand for the base. Add in charges for hauling away excess dirt and renting tools like a power sod cutter and a plate vibrator or compactor to tamp down the pavers once they have been laid.

Pavers and Base Materials

Home and garden centers stock paving bricks in a range of colors and shapes. Take along a sketch of the plans for your patio to help in estimating the quantity of materials you will need. Don't consider pavers less than 2-1/2 inches thick. Once you have made your final choice, ask a salesperson to help you calculate how many bricks you'll need and the length of plastic edging required for the perimeter of your patio. If possible, arrange for delivery to your home, because patio materials are heavy and you'll probably find the extra cost worth it.

For the crushed rock and sand you'll need for the patio's base, look in your telephone Yellow Pages under "Sand." Again, have it delivered if possible. Try to find Class 5 limestone for crushed rock, which compacts well and makes an excellent base material. You don't need anything better than coarse, unwashed sand—it works even better than the finer and more expensive types of sand for this application.

Crushed rock and sand are sold by the cubic yard. To determine how much you'll need, use this formula:

[Length (ft.) x width (ft.) x depth (ft.)] ÷ 27 = Cubic yds.

For the crushed rock for this 20x17-foot patio, for example:

[20 ft. x 17 ft. x .3 (for a rock depth of 3 1/2 in.)] ÷ 27 = 3.77 or 4 cubic yds.

Skills and Tools

This patio isn't difficult to build and requires only ordinary hand tools, for the most part: round-point and square-point spades, a wheelbarrow, a blacksmith's hammer or small maul, a large broom, a string line, a level, wooden stakes, a hacksaw, two lengths of 1-1/8 inch outside-diameter (O.D.) steel pipe to guide the screed, a screwdriver, and a measuring tape.

You can rent the few specialized tools you'll need: a power sod cutter, a masonry saw, and a 24-inch plate compactor. Always use hearing protection and wear safety goggles when you operate a masonry saw.

Tools You Need

Hand Tools

Blacksmith's hammer or small maul

Carpenter's pencil

Hacksaw

Hearing protection, safety goggles

Large broom

Level

Round-point and square-point spades

Screed pipes

Screwdrivers

Stakes and string line

Tape measure

Wheelbarrow

Power Tools

Masonry saw (rented)

Plate compactor (rented)

Sod cutter (rented)

Plastic edging cuts easily
with a hacksaw. To
achieve smooth-flowing
curves, avoid placing
splices anywhere the
edging bends.

Prepare the Base

The first stage in preparing the base is to lay out the perimeter of your patio.

▶ Begin by staking out the overall outline. Then use stakes and string to mark borders 8 inches beyond the perimeter. Mark the outer borders with spray paint (Photo 1). The crushed-rock base you will be laying will extend out to this border to support the edges of the patio.

Decide now if you will want to include the sunscreen pergola. If so, and if you want to attach it to the house, prepare footings for it. They should extend at least 6 inches below the frost line in your area (the local building inspector can tell you how deep that is). See the Pergola Construction Plan on page 112 and Build a Solid Foundation on pages 16–17.

▶ Remove the sod with a sod cutter, then roll it up (Photo 2). Store the rolls in a cool location. If you can't reuse them within three days you'll have to discard them. To avoid damaging your lawn, don't leave dirt and sod on it for more than a few days.

▶ Excavate the base area to 7 inches below the sod, to allow 3-1/2 inches for the rock base, 1 inch for the sand, and 2-1/2 inches for the pavers. Level the soil with a square-point spade (Photo 3).

▶ Drive at least three stakes on each side of the patio and down its center. Align them carefully—they'll support the pipe screed guides later. Use a level and a long 2x4 to mark the depth of the crushed rock on the stakes. The rock should be at least 3-1/2 inches deep (Photo 4). Now cut each stake 1-1/8 inches below the line marking the rock depth. This will place the top of the screed guide pipes at the height of the rock bed. Place the pipes on the stakes and secure them with screws (Photo 5).

▶ Spread the crushed rock fairly evenly with a shovel, then use a long 2x4 to screed it level with the tops of the pipe guides. If you're building a large patio, it's best to do just half the area at a time (Photo 6). Once the crushed-rock base is level, remove the pipes and fill any voids.

▶ Move the plate compactor to the patio area, which is a two-person job. Before you start the engine, make sure you have a firm grip on the machine. You'll need a bit of practice before being able to control its direction. Fill voids and make multiple passes over the entire area until the crushed rock feels firm underfoot (Photo 7).

▶ Now reset your stakes-and-string border to the final dimensions of the finished patio. Align the edging under the string, and then secure it with stakes every 8 inches. You can fine-tune the position of the edging later.

▶ To achieve an even 1-inch sand base on top of the crushed rock, lay a length of pipe across the middle of the rock (Photo 8). Then cut a notch in the 2x4 screed so it will ride 1 inch above the base of the edging. Spread sand over the area and screed it smooth. Start at one end and level half the patio at a time. Remove the pipe and fill any small voids with sand, smoothing the surface with a section of 2x4.

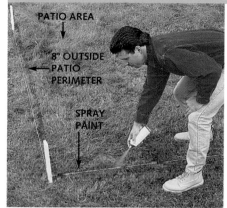

Photo 1. Use spray paint to mark a line 8 in. beyond the patio's perimeter. Crushed rock will extend that far to support the patio's edges.

Photo 2. Remove the sod with a power sod cutter like the one shown here or a manual kick-type cutter, both available for rental.

Photo 3. Excavate the patio area to about 7 in. below the sod. Remove the dirt to a location from which it will be easy to haul away.

Photo 4. Mark the depth of the crushed rock on stakes driven along the perimeter and in the middle of the patio.

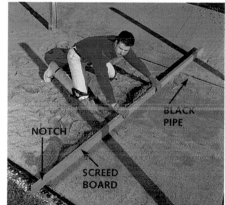

Photo 5. Screw the pipes firmly to the stakes. The top of each stake must be 1-1/8 in. below the final height of the crushed rock.

Photo 6. Screed crushed rock to an even depth, using a long 2x4. The screed pipes act as guides. Do a wide patio by halves.

Photo 7. Compress the crushed rock with a power compactor. Check the base with a level and a long 2x4, fill voids, and compact again.

Photo 8. Level the sand, using the pipes as a guide. Notch the 2x4 end that rides along the edging so the board is level.

Lay the Pavers

This patio incorporates a contrasting border for visual interest. Here's how to add a border like the one shown.

Positioning the Pavers

▶ First, lay the first pavers along a straight side of the patio or adjoining the house. Install enough border pavers to establish the pattern before you begin to fill the patio area. Lay half sheets of plywood over the sand to support your own weight and that of the pavers (Photo 9).

▶ Instead of trying to beat the pavers into place with a mallet, simply place them on the sand base and keep them butted tightly against each other. Wait until all the full-sized pavers are in place before doing any cutting. If you need to reposition some of the edging, pull up the stakes, push the edging up snug against the pavers, and reinstall the stakes.

Cutting the Pavers

▶ To cut brick pavers, rent a masonry saw. It will be heavy and awkward to maneuver, so recruit a helper to load it into your car and to carry it to the work site. Always make sure there is water in the saw's reservoir. Use face and hearing protection whenever you operate one of these saws (Photo 10).

▶ With a carpenter's pencil, mark each paver to be cut. Then trim and fit the bricks one at a time (Photo 11).

LAY THE PAVERS

Photo 9. Lay the pavers on top of the sand, using a string line as a guide. Use scrap plywood to support the weight of you and the pavers.

Photo 10. A masonry saw is a powerful piece of equipment. Always wear face and ear protection when operating one.

Photo 11. After all the field pavers are in place, mark cut lines for any outer, irregular pavers. Then cut the pavers with a masonry saw.

Finishing Touches

After all the outer pavers have been cut and placed, run the plate compactor over the entire surface to settle the pavers (Photo 12). If one particular paver has sunk or is sitting too high, pry it out with a screwdriver, and add or remove a bit of sand.

Shake more coarse, dry sand over the entire patio, working it back and forth in all directions with a large broom (Photo 13).

Brush in more sand periodically over the next few weeks as natural settling occurs.

Brick pavers typically don't need to be protected from the elements. If you like, however, you can apply a water sealant designed specifically for bricks and concrete. To complete the patio, fill the area around the edging with dirt. Then spread grass seed or reinstall the sod you originally removed, to reestablish the lawn.

FINISHING TOUCHES

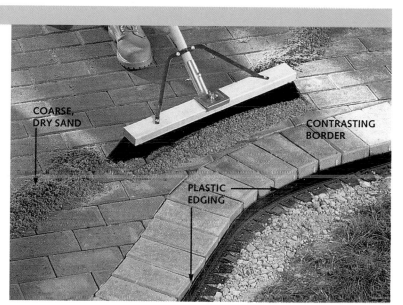

COARSE, DRY SAND

CONTRASTING BORDER

PLASTIC EDGING

Photo 12. Use a mechanical plate compactor to help settle the pavers. The compactor will also level any unevenness in the surface.

Photo 13. Sweep sand into the spaces between the pavers, then use the mechanical compactor over the entire surface one last time.

Pergola Construction Plan

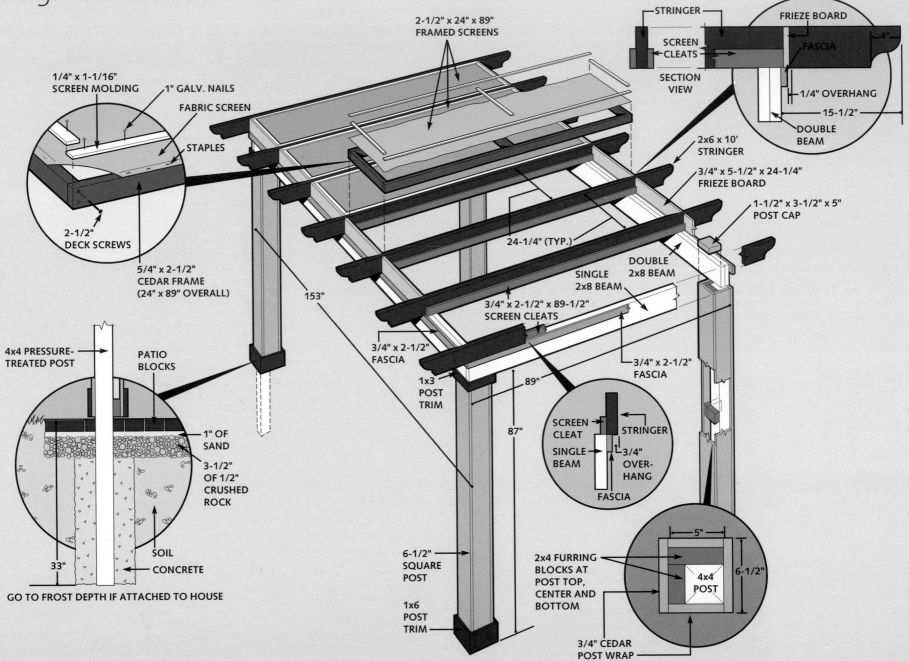

1/4" x 1-1/16" SCREEN MOLDING

1" GALV. NAILS

FABRIC SCREEN

STAPLES

2-1/2" DECK SCREWS

5/4" x 2-1/2" CEDAR FRAME (24" x 89" OVERALL)

2-1/2" x 24" x 89" FRAMED SCREENS

STRINGER

SCREEN CLEATS

SECTION VIEW

FRIEZE BOARD

FASCIA

4"

1/4" OVERHANG

15-1/2"

DOUBLE BEAM

2x6 x 10' STRINGER

3/4" x 5-1/2" x 24-1/4" FRIEZE BOARD

1-1/2" x 3-1/2" x 5" POST CAP

24-1/4" (TYP.)

DOUBLE 2x8 BEAM

SINGLE 2x8 BEAM

3/4" x 2-1/2" x 89-1/2" SCREEN CLEATS

3/4" x 2-1/2" FASCIA

153"

3/4" x 2-1/2" FASCIA

1x3 POST TRIM

89"

4x4 PRESSURE-TREATED POST

PATIO BLOCKS

1" OF SAND

3-1/2" OF 1/2" CRUSHED ROCK

SOIL

CONCRETE

33"

GO TO FROST DEPTH IF ATTACHED TO HOUSE

87"

SCREEN CLEAT

SINGLE BEAM

STRINGER

3/4" OVER-HANG

FASCIA

6-1/2" SQUARE POST

1x6 POST TRIM

2x4 FURRING BLOCKS AT POST TOP, CENTER AND BOTTOM

5"

4x4 POST

6-1/2"

3/4" CEDAR POST WRAP

The Sunscreen Pergola

The sunscreen fabric of this pergola blocks 60 to 70 percent of the sun's rays, and its decorative stringers provide their own shade as the angle of the sun changes throughout the day. Best of all, this pergola is so simple that if you've tackled even the most basic of carpentry projects you can build this one with ease.

Plan Your Sunscreen Pergola

This pergola was built over the brick paver patio just constructed, but it would work every bit as well over a ground-level deck, a concrete slab, or even a layer of creek-bed stones or wood chips.

Tools and Time

You'll need only such basic power tools as a circular saw and a saber saw to build this pergola. You should also have available a hammer, a handsaw, scissors, a staple gun with 5/16-inch staples, a tape measure, a string line, a level, a wheelbarrow or tub for mixing the concrete, and two 6-foot ladders. A rented 8-inch power auger will also come in handy, since the postholes will be deeper than is usual for footings.

Unlike some deck and porch projects that can take most of a summer to build, you can complete this pergola in just two or three weekends. Be aware, however, that the materials are heavy, so have them delivered if at all possible.

Erect the Posts

▶ Before you dig holes for the four 4x4 pressure-treated posts that support this structure, check with your local utility companies to make sure no underground lines are in the way. Then dig postholes that are at least 30 inches deep and 8 inches wide. (In some areas it may be necessary to dig below the frost line.)

▶ Lay out the perimeter of your pergola with stakes and string. Locate and dig the holes as shown in the Pergola Construction Plan on the facing page. Once the posts have been centered in their holes, align their outside faces exactly with the corners of your perimeter layout.

▶ Mix the concrete to a firm consistency. Plan on using at least one and one-half 60-pound bags of dry-mix concrete for each hole. Position the posts, bracing them with 1x3's or scrap lumber to square them up, then pour the concrete around them.

▶ Double-check that each post is square with the perimeter layout. Use a level to find plumb. Let the concrete set overnight.

▶ To mark the posts for cutting, use a level and a long, straight board. Because your pergola probably won't be on perfectly level ground, measure the post height at the highest point, then transfer the marks to the other posts. Use a circular saw to cut the posts off level at the marks, finishing with a handsaw as needed.

▶ Now cut 2x4 furring blocks for the inside corners and nail them to the posts at the top, center, and bottom as shown in the Pergola Construction Plan. Then wrap the posts with cedar facing (Photo 14). Check the actual width of each post. Because the size of 4x4's can vary, you may need to cut some boards a bit wider than shown.

Photo 14. To give the posts the look of columns, wrap them with 3/4-in. cedar after nailing on furring blocks.

Tools You Need

Hand Tools

Hammer and nail set

Handsaw

Level

Measuring tape

Mixing tub or wheelbarrow

Posthole digger

Scissors

Screwdriver

Staple gun (5/16 in.)

Stakes and string line

Tape measure

Two 6-ft. ladders

Power Tools

Drill

Circular saw

Saber saw

Optional

8-in. auger (rented)

Power screwdriver

Build the Roof

After the cedar post wraps are in place, install the roof.

▶ Cut the single 2x8 end beams to the outside dimensions of the posts. Measure the distance between the single beams, then cut the double 2x8 beams to butt snugly between them (see the Pergola Construction Plan on page 112). Position the beams to form a box that fits flush with the outside edges of the wrapped posts. Nail a post cap to the column tops inside the beam corners. Join the double beam members with 16d galvanized box nails and place the double beams on the columns. Nail the double beams to a single beam at each end (Photo 15). Nail the single beams into the post caps and toenail their corners into the 4x4.

▶ Measure and cut the posts' trim pieces to size. Nail the 1x6 sections to the bottom of each column, then the 1x3 pieces to the top. Measure and cut the fascias and nail them to the single and double beams (see page 112).

▶ Using a saber saw, cut decorative scallops on the ends of each 10-foot 2x6 stringer (Photo 16). Lift them onto the tops of the beams, spaced evenly (Photo 17). To support the end stringers, toenail them from outside to the single beams. Position the stringers to overhang the fascia by 1/2 inch along the single beams. Space the interior stringers evenly. Toenail them to the double beams with 16d galvanized box nails.

▶ Measure and cut the frieze boards to fit between the stringers. Let these boards overhang the fascias by 1/4 inch. Toenail the frieze boards to the stringers and double beams with 8d galvanized nails.

BUILD THE ROOF

Photo 15. Install the beams on top of the columns. Nail the single beams to the longer double beams and toenail their corners to the post caps.

Photo 16. Cut the decorative scalloped curves on each end of the 10-ft. 2x6 stringers with a saber saw after installing the trim.

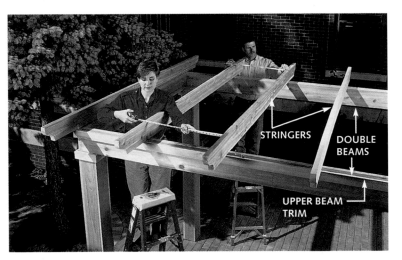

Photo 17. Space the stringers evenly so the sunscreen frames are identical. Toenail the stringers to the double beams.

Make the Sunscreens

The last step before applying a finish to your new pergola is to construct the sunscreens, if you choose to.

▶ Measure the distance between the stringers. Then cut the outside members of the sunscreen frames 1/4 inch shorter, to make installation easier and allow for wood's natural expansion. For the same reasons, cut the long frame members at least 1/2 inch shorter than the distance between the frieze boards. Use 2-1/2 inch galvanized deck screws to assemble the frames as shown in the top left detail in the Pergola Construction Plan on page 112.

▶ Cut six pieces of sunscreen fabric to the outside dimensions of the frames. Use a staple gun and 5/16-inch staples every 1-1/2 inches to attach the fabric to the tops of the frames, pulling the fabric taut from side to side (Photo 18). If you plan to stain or seal the wood, apply the finish before the fabric.

▶ Measure and cut lengths of screen molding to cover the top edges of the frames completely. Then nail the screen molding to the wooden frames with 1-inch galvanized nails (Photo 19).

▶ Cut the twelve screen cleats, which in this design are 89 1/2 inches long, and attach them to the stringers with 8d galvanized casing nails (Photo 20).

▶ Set the screens in place on top of the screen cleats. If winters are severe in your area and you'll need to remove the screens seasonally, use hook-and-eye fasteners to attach the frames to the cleats. Otherwise, screw the frames to the cleats from above with 3-1/2 inch galvanized deck screws.

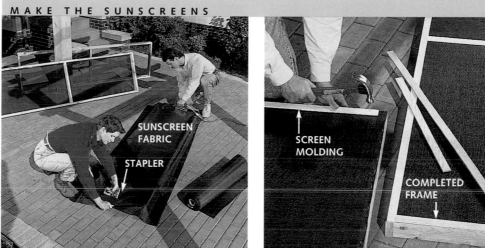

Photo 18. Staple the sunscreen to the frames every 1-1/2 in. Stain or seal the wood first.

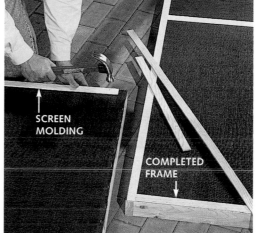

Photo 19. Nail the screen molding to the frames with 1-in. galvanized nails.

Finishing Tip

To keep the wood of your pergola looking like it was freshly cut, apply an exterior semitransparent oil stain. If you prefer a weathered look, leave the wood unfinished.

Photo 20. Nail the screen-frame cleats to the stringers, then set the frames into each opening.

Patio First Aid

The patio is probably one of your home's most popular gathering spots.

But if its timber edging has heaved out of place, its bricks have started to dip,

or its blocks have begun to crumble, you're probably not enjoying it as

much as you could. Here's how to repair and restore patios made of paver

bricks or 8x12-inch patio blocks.

Removing an old, deteriorated timber border and replacing it with new weather-resistant preformed plastic edging is a lasting, simple repair.

Repair Paver-Brick Edging

When paver bricks first became popular in the late 1970s, the methods used to retain the outside rows of pavers weren't as refined as they are today. Most of those early patio installations used treated lumber as borders, in every size from 2x4's to 6x6's. But it took only a few years of ground movement from winter freeze-thaw cycles before the timbers—and often a few of the outside rows of bricks—heaved out of position.

Today, patios made of pavers use pre-formed plastic edging that holds the bricks tightly in place. Although this improved edging may cost more than replacement timbers, once you've installed it the edges will be virtually maintenance-free.

Besides the new plastic edging, you'll need some coarse sand, probably some topsoil, and most likely a roll or two of sod to fill areas that were originally covered by the timbers. Don't plan to reuse any old sod you take up unless you do so within three days.

Removing old timbers and installing new edging is labor intensive, but the job shouldn't take longer than a day or so from start to finish.

▶ Remove the old timbers. Don't be surprised if both pieces at a corner come up as one unit. They're probably nailed together with foot-long spikes.

▶ You'll probably need to remove at least one row of pavers as well (Photo 1).

▶ Add coarse sand to form a base for the new edging and the pavers. Use a short length of 2x4 to smooth the sand, then check its height by placing a paver on the sand. This paver should stick up between 1/2 and 3/4 inch above the surface of the surrounding pavers (Photo 2).

▶ Tamp down the added sand with a tamping tool. If you don't want to rent one, you can make a perfectly workable tamper out of two one-foot squares of 3/4-inch plywood nailed to a 2x4. Make sure the entire sand base has been evenly tamped, so you won't have to add sand later to level the pavers (Photo 3).

▶ Check the height of the pavers with a level. Adjust the base now so that all the pavers are even and level (Photo 4).

▶ Reinstall the pavers, then insert the plastic edging. Remember to follow the pavers' design and pattern. Install all the pavers before securing the edging with its metal anchoring stakes. Follow the edging manufacturer's instructions for spacing out the metal anchoring stakes (Photo 5).

▶ Add topsoil to level the areas where timber was removed. Cut a strip of sod and lay it in place. Keep the sod watered. Don't cut or trim it for at least four weeks (Photo 6).

Tools You Need

Hand Tools

Pickax

Shovel

Tamping tool

Three-lb. maul

Two-ft. level

Optional

Mechanical vibrating tamper (rented)

Photo 1. Remove old timbers with a pickax. Start at the end of one of the timbers and pry it up gradually, working down its length.

Photo 2. Add coarse sand, then level it and check its height by placing a paver on it. The paver should stick up 1/2 to 3/4 in. above other pavers.

Photo 3. Tamp down the added sand with a tamping tool. Make sure the entire sand base has been compressed, so you won't have to add sand later.

Photo 4. Check the height of the pavers with a level. Adjust the sand base now so that the pavers are uniformly even and level.

Photo 5. Reinstall the pavers and insert the plastic edging. Install all the pavers before securing the edging with the metal anchoring stakes.

Photo 6. Add topsoil to level the area where timber was removed. Cut a strip of sod and lay it in place. Water often, but don't cut it for four weeks.

Level Dips and Heaves

Even the most carefully installed and maintained patios can fall victim to the ravages of nature. Rain may wash out the sand base, causing the bricks to sink, and tree roots can surface, pushing up bricks in the process.

To level sunken pavers, follow these steps.
▶ Remove one of the sunken bricks, using two long-shaft screwdrivers (Photo 7). Pry out the paver a bit at a time by inching the screwdrivers down on opposite sides.
▶ Carefully pry out additional pavers until you can remove the remaining sunken bricks by hand. Take care not to break any of the paver bricks, especially if you don't have any spares to replace them.
▶ Add enough coarse sand to the sunken areas of the base to bring it back up to its original even level.
▶ Reinstall the bricks and spread additional sand with a broom to fill any gaps that occur between the bricks.

Reinstalling the pavers can be frustrating, because of their interlocking design (Photo 8). To make the last few pavers fit, wiggle them in as far as you can. Then lay a short 2x4 on each paver and use a 3-pound maul to tap it down until it's level.

If the pavers have heaved, you'll need to eliminate the cause of the problem. In this particular case, the heaving was caused by a 2-inch diameter tree root (Photo 9).

Resist the temptation simply to cut out a root that has surfaced, because you risk killing the tree. If the root is large enough, however, you may be able to shave it down without harming the tree. Check with a nursery for the best approach to solving your root problem.

Tools You Need

Hand Tools

Garden fork or shovel

Garden hose with spray nozzle

Two long-shafted screwdrivers

Optional

Power washer (rented)

LEVEL DIPS AND HEAVES

LONG-SHAFTED SCREWDRIVERS

Photo 7. Slip the tips of long-shafted screwdrivers along the opposite ends of a paver until you can pry it up enough to remove it by hand.

INTERLOCKED PAVER

Photo 8. Removing interlocking pavers is slow work, so be patient. The first few bricks will have to be removed with a pair of screwdrivers.

SHAVED TREE ROOT

Photo 9. Reinstall the pavers after you've corrected the alignment problem. After the bricks are in place, spread coarse sand with a broom to fill the joints.

Clean and Repair Patio Blocks

Not long ago, 8x12-inch patio blocks were as common as paver bricks today. But even though they're less popular now, patio blocks are still sold at most home centers and landscape-supply stores.

Most problems that patio blocks exhibit are related to their high porosity: in addition to their ability to retain water, they also hold a lot of dirt and sand. Fortunately, cleaning them is easy. Simply spray the blocks with a garden hose, scrub them with a stiff-bristled broom such as one for a garage, and hose them off again.

If the blocks have become too dirty to clean properly with a garden hose, rent a power washer. Its high-pressure stream will blast away a small amount of the block's surface as it also removes dirt and sand. Look for a power washer with a pressure range of 1,200 to 2,500 pounds per square inch (you may find it worthwhile, as long as you have the washer rented already, to go ahead and power wash your sidewalks and driveway for good measure).

Patio blocks can become pitted after exposure to a constant stream of water, such as runoff from a house or garage roof. After a few years the water will cut a groove in the blocks' surface. The easiest way to solve this problem is to hide it, simply by flipping the blocks over (Photo 10). Turning a block over will expose a new surface that should last as long as the side that was worn out.

▶ Remove three of the patio blocks, using a shovel or garden fork. Lay them aside.
▶ Now remove the fourth block, flip it over, and lay it in the spot from which the first block was removed.
▶ Add coarse sand under each block as needed for leveling.
▶ Keep repeating this "remove, flip, and replace" process until all the blocks have been turned over.
▶ Finally, hose or scrub the dirt off the newly turned blocks.

Replacing a cracked patio block is much easier than substituting one interlocking paver for another. You can readily remove damaged blocks by hand. And because new patio blocks are still available in the same shades of red, green, and gold that were sold years ago, you should be able to match the block's color closely.

Photo 10. Remove, flip over, and replace blocks with a garden fork as needed. Add coarse sand under the blocks as required, then hose off new surfaces.

Remove Moss and Mildew

To remove moss and mildew from your paver patio, mix 1 quart of household bleach to 3 quarts of water. Pour this solution over the bricks and scrub it in with a stiff-bristled broom. Then rinse the bricks with a garden hose.

To prevent regrowth of the moss or mildew, try to keep excess moisture off your patio bricks and expose them to as much sunlight as the site allows. If that's not possible, resign yourself to repeating this procedure from time to time. Moss and mildew aren't serious problems, but they can be slippery as well as unsightly.

Porches

Classic Front Porch   **124**

You'll love sipping lemonade on this splendid porch. A project for the experienced DIYer, it will take lots of planning and work. But the reward is a place to relax for years and years to come.

Classic Front Porch

A carpenter may tell you that a front porch is just a floor with a roof over it and a railing

around it, but any homeowner will tell you that a porch is much more.

It's a hideaway from the hubbub inside the house, a place for swapping fish stories

with the next-door neighbor, a haven for reading or knitting, a spot for nodding off

on a lazy summer afternoon, or a venue for lively parties.

If you decide to build this classic front porch, be prepared to invest several

hundred hours in a complex and involved project. But in return you'll be

rewarded with a place to relax for years to come, and you'll have a substantial

addition to your home.

The porch in the photo on the right looks like it has been here as long as the original house on the left—because its roof follows the same angle as the house roof, its siding and shutters match those of the house, and its turned railing spindles and knot-free wrapped posts blend right in with the design of the house.

Construction Plan

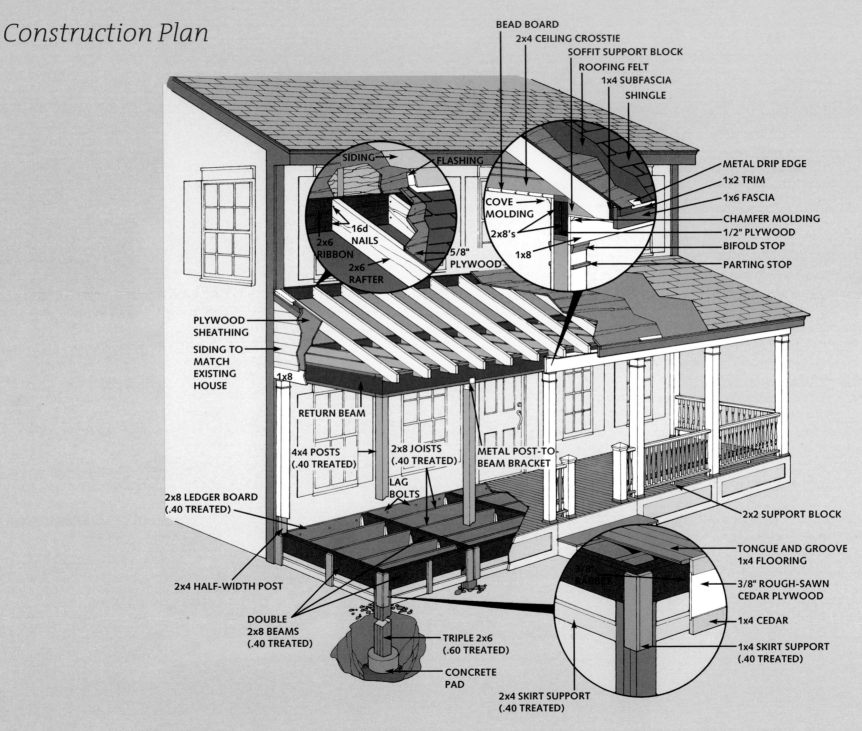

BEAD BOARD
2x4 CEILING CROSSTIE
SOFFIT SUPPORT BLOCK
ROOFING FELT
1x4 SUBFASCIA
SHINGLE

METAL DRIP EDGE
1x2 TRIM
1x6 FASCIA
CHAMFER MOLDING
1/2" PLYWOOD
BIFOLD STOP
PARTING STOP

SIDING
FLASHING
COVE MOLDING
2x8's
1x8

16d NAILS
2x6 RIBBON
2x6 RAFTER
5/8" PLYWOOD

PLYWOOD SHEATHING
SIDING TO MATCH EXISTING HOUSE
1x8
RETURN BEAM

4x4 POSTS (.40 TREATED)
2x8 JOISTS (.40 TREATED)
METAL POST-TO-BEAM BRACKET
LAG BOLTS

2x8 LEDGER BOARD (.40 TREATED)

2x2 SUPPORT BLOCK

TONGUE AND GROOVE 1x4 FLOORING
3/8" ROUGH-SAWN CEDAR PLYWOOD
1x4 CEDAR
1x4 SKIRT SUPPORT (.40 TREATED)

3/8" RABBET

2x4 HALF-WIDTH POST

DOUBLE 2x8 BEAMS (.40 TREATED)
TRIPLE 2x6 (.60 TREATED)
CONCRETE PAD
2x4 SKIRT SUPPORT (.40 TREATED)

Plan Your Classic Front Porch

With a project of this size and scope, make sure to analyze thoroughly the various planning and construction factors before you start to build.

Design Considerations

This shed-roof or single-pitch porch is ideal for a two-story house. The slope of the porch roof mimics that of the house roof, and the roof intersects the house between the first- and second-story windows. It would be difficult, however, to adapt this type of shed-roof porch to a single-story home. If you have a one-story house you should probably opt for a porch design with a gable-end roof like the one shown in "Rambler Front Porch" (page 138).

The owners of the home pictured here hired an architect to design their porch. Unless your home is identical, you should consider hiring professional design help also. The style of your house, the pitch of its roof, and the details of the eaves will all affect your porch's final design and dimensions. There are few architectural mistakes worse than a porch that appears tacked on or that is incompatible with the overall style of your home.

It is important to think of your house and your new porch as a package: the roof pitch, the distance between the upper and lower windows, the width of the porch, and the height of the porch support posts all affect one another.

▶ To visualize the relationship of the new porch to the rest of the house, sketch your design on graph paper. First draw a horizontal line straight out from the top of your first-story windows, to represent your porch ceiling. Then draw a line slanting down from the bottom of the second-story windows at the same angle as the house roof. The point at which these lines intersect will determine the maximum width of your porch. The steeper the roof's pitch or the smaller the distance between the first- and second-floor windows, the narrower your porch will have to be.

▶ Factor in the height of the support beam, the slope of the floor, the length of the front overhang, local building-code specifications for all the structural members, and the design details that will allow the porch to blend as seamlessly as possible with the prevailing style of your house. Again, with the success of your porch dependent upon so many variables, it's wise to hire the services of an architect.

▶ Provide your architect with actual samples of the styles of spindles and railings you like, along with magazine clippings of posts, skirts, and other porch details that you've found attractive. This will allow him or her to incorporate these elements into the detailed drawings of your porch.

Pay special attention to the spacing of the support columns. The windows and doors of the house pictured here happen to be evenly spaced, which allowed for regularly spaced columns along the front of the porch that do not interfere with the view out any window. If your house lacks such symmetry, you'll need to seek out a compromise between the appearance of the columns' spacing and its effect on your view.

Tools You Need

Hand Tools

Batter boards and string
Caulk
Chalk line
4-ft. level
Framing square
Hacksaw
Handsaw
Hoe
Mallet
Hammers
Nail set
Pliers
Posthole digger
Pry bar
Screwdrivers
Shovel
Socket wrench
Stepladders
Tape measure
Utility knife
Wheelbarrow

Power Tools

Circular saw
Drill
8-in. auger
Miter saw
Router
Bench saw or radial arm saw

Skill Level

This project is immensely complex and involved, appropriate only for the most experienced of do-it-yourselfers. The design involves a multitude of details and measurements that must be absolutely correct. A miscalculation in any one of them can cause fitting and assembly problems further down the line. To describe all the details of its construction would fill a book on its own. This chapter describes the principal steps and provides some pro tips for executing the details properly. Even with good blueprints, this porch proved so challenging for the experienced do-it-yourself owners of this home that it proved worth calling in professional carpenters to handle some of the unplanned surprises that came up. The project took more than 150 hours to complete the carpentry work and another 40 hours to do the painting.

However, some of the work is repetitive. For example, one tongue-and-groove deck board goes down much like the next. The same is true of building the trusses, installing the ceiling bead board, and putting in the railings. So even if you're not a skilled carpenter, you may be able to do some of the work yourself and hire professional carpenters for the rest.

Materials

This porch was built with only first-class materials: clear, knot-free fir for the floor boards, clear southern yellow pine for the ceiling, and decorative spindles for the railings. Using lower grades of lumber or different species of wood is not recommended if you want this porch to endure years of exposure to the elements and heavy foot traffic and remain an attractive entry point to your home. An investment in high-quality materials will prove to be money well spent.

Building-Code Requirements

Before proceeding further, check with a local building inspector to discover the setback regulations in your community. Many areas require a 30- to 50-foot distance between a lot's front boundary line and any additions to the house. If your proposed porch infringes on this setback distance you'll need to apply for a zoning variance, a process that can be lengthy and expensive. You can improve your chances of being granted a variance by presenting well-thought-out plans designed with the help of an architect.

Stoop Considerations

The owners of the home in this project were able to build their porch floor directly over an existing concrete stoop. If your stoop is at least 4 inches below the bottom of your front door, and preferably a full step below it, you may elect to do the same (see Photo 3).

If you choose to build your porch floor over an existing stoop, make certain that its footings extend below the frost line for your area so it won't move during freeze-thaw cycles. Otherwise it could heave and ruin the floor of your new porch.

Build Your Classic Front Porch

Lay Out the Porch

After you have obtained all the required building permits and made the final changes to the blueprints, you're ready to begin excavating the site. Before you do, however, ask your local utility companies to examine the site and mark the paths of any underground electrical and plumbing connections.

▶ Next, remove the siding where the porch floor will connect to the house. Use batter boards and string to lay out and square up the perimeter of the porch (Photo 1).

▶ Now snap a level chalk line the length of the house, leaving enough room for the tongue-and-groove decking to slide under the door threshold and siding. Then lag-bolt a pressure-treated ledger board to the house along this line.

▶ You have several options for constructing the footings that will support the porch floor. For a discussion of good and better footings, see pages 16–17. For this project, dig a series of holes below frost depth along the front of the porch. Then pour an 8-inch thick concrete footing pad in the bottom and install extra-long, triple-2x6, .60-rated treated posts designed for below-ground use (see the Construction Plan on page 126). At this point, use the ledger as a guide to mark level lines on the corner posts. Drop the marks 1 inch to provide a slope for the floor (Photo 2). Then snap a chalk line from one end post to the other to mark the height of the intermediate posts. Finally, cut all the posts to the correct height with a circular saw. Finish with a handsaw if necessary.

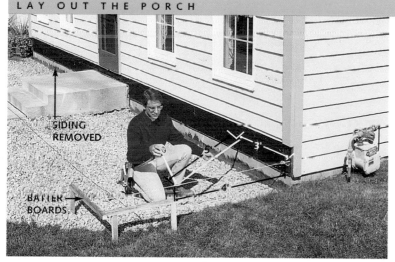

LAY OUT THE PORCH

SIDING REMOVED

BATTER BOARDS

Photo 1. Lay out the perimeter with batter boards and string. Check for square using a 3–4–5 triangle (see page 95). Dig footing holes, pour concrete, and install the posts.

LEDGER BOARD

FLOOR SUPPORT POST

MARK POST LEVEL, THEN DROP MARK 1" TO CREATE FLOOR SLOPE

Photo 2. Mark lines on the two end posts level with the bottom of the ledger board. Lower both marks 1 in. to slope the floor, snap chalk lines to mark intermediate posts, and cut the posts.

Construct the Floor

When porches fail, rotted floors and posts usually are at fault. A well-constructed porch floor should include the following lines of defense against rot and the elements.

▶ Use treated lumber whenever possible. Tongue-and-groove 3/4 x 3-inch vertical-grain fir boards are recommended for flooring. This porch uses .60 treated lumber, rated for below-ground use, for the floor-support posts. It also has .40 treated lumber, rated for wood that will make ground contact, for the floor beams, joists, and roof-support posts.

▶ Make sure the porch floor is angled so that it sheds water. This particular porch slopes 1 inch for each 6 feet in depth. Its deck boards also run parallel to the slope, for better drainage.

▶ Shim between the stoop and the ripped-down joists to add strength where the joists cross the stoop (Photo 3).

▶ Protect all four sides of each of the tongue-and-groove deck boards with an oil-base primer to seal out water (Photo 4). Alternatively, soak the flooring in preservative prior to laying it. Then apply a bead of latex painter's caulk in each groove as you install the boards (Photo 5).

▶ Allow for air circulation. Make sure that the lumber will be able to dry out if your other precautions fail. This porch incorporates a 3/4-inch space behind the skirt boards and a 2- to 3-inch gap below the skirt boards so air can circulate freely beneath the floor (see bottom right detail of the Construction Plan on page 126).

As you build the floor, keep in mind the following points.

▶ Use only galvanized nails and fasteners. Although they are more expensive, the hot-dipped type are the best. For a large project you may find it worth renting a power nailer. They are easy, if tedious, to use. Just slip a board into position, fit the nailer over its tongue, and hit it with a mallet.

▶ To minimize squeaking, apply construction adhesive to secure the floor boards to the joists (Photo 6).

▶ As you lay the deck boards, let them extend over the edges, then snap a chalk line 3/4 inch beyond the beam and cut the boards all together along this line (Photo 7).

Photo 3. Install the floor joists with their curved or crowned edges up. Doubled beams support single 2x8's. If you leave a stoop, rip joists to width at that point and shim them level.

Photo 4. Apply oil-base primer to all four sides of the tongue-and-groove floor boards, to protect them from moisture and rot. Do this before installing the boards.

Photo 5. Run a bead of latex painter's caulk in the groove of each floor board before installing it. The best time to rot- and moistureproof your porch floor is as you build it.

CONSTRUCTION
ADHESIVE

TOENAIL

Photo 6. Install the deck boards by blind-nailing through the upper edges of the tongues into the joists. Apply construction adhesive between the deck boards and joists for a solid, squeak-free floor.

3/4"
OVERHANG

CHALK
LINE

Photo 7. Cut the floor boards to length, letting them extend 3/4 in. past the front beam. When all the boards are in place, snap a chalk line as a guide to use in cutting them.

Build the Roof

Even though your blueprints may show theoretical measurements for the posts and rafters, you'll be working on a real house with variations in the trueness of the existing walls, lumber dimensions, and porch-floor height. To minimize your work, start by building one roof truss, with the pitch of the rafter mimicking that of the existing roof and the crosstie being the same length as the depth of the porch. Include a spacer board to represent the rafter and ceiling ribbons (Photos 8 and 12).

▶ Nail this model truss to the house, level the ceiling crosstie, and use a story stick to determine the posts' height (Photo 8). Do this on both ends and in the middle, then determine the average height. Subtract the height of your beam to determine the actual post height. Make any changes in the length or angle of the truss member at this time. Use the ends of this truss as a guide to mark the location of the 2x4 and 2x6 ribbons. Then snap chalk lines and nail these ribbons to the wall studs of the house.

▶ While the porch floor is still wide open, build the roof trusses (Photo 9). Take apart the model truss, then use its three components as patterns to trace and cut the remaining pieces. Nail the trusses together and set them aside for now.

▶ Toenail the roof-support posts to the floor, then carefully plumb and brace them as shown in Photo 10. Nail the post-to-beam brackets on top of the intermediate posts. Remove a narrow strip of siding from the corners of the house and nail on two 2x4's there to act as half posts.

▶ Build the beam, sandwiching lengths of 1/2-inch plywood between 2x8 members. Stagger the ends of the 2x8 boards so that they rest on alternating posts (see the Construction Plan on page 126). With at least two helpers, lift the beam onto the posts and brackets (Photo 11). Also install the return beams, which run between the corner posts and the house as shown in the Construction Plan.

▶ Nail on the roof trusses, positioning them every 2 feet center to center (Photo 12). Then nail 5/8-inch plywood roof sheathing to the trusses and install the fascias and drip edges to finish the edges of the roof.

▶ Tuck lengths of flashing up and behind the siding where the roof meets the vertical face of the house just under the second-story windows. Then tuck roofing felt or a polyethylene film in under the flashing. Finally, shingle the roof, tucking the last row of shingles under the flashing.

As you are building the roof, remember to do the following.

▶ Leave at least 1-1/2 inches of space below the second-story windows so that the flashing will be easy to install (Photo 13). In wintry climates you may want to leave even more space to prevent snow from building up against the windows.

▶ If the wall of the house bows in or out or is otherwise out of plumb, shim behind the 2x6 rafter ribbon to straighten it.

▶ Duplicate the home's existing soffit and fascia details in the design for the porch.

Photo 8. Determine the posts' height by using a sample roof truss and a story stick. The top of the 2x6 rafter should be far enough below the windows to allow for sheathing, flashing, and shingles.

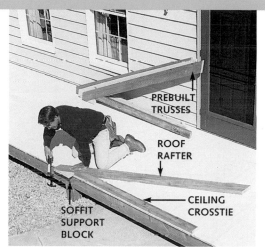

Photo 9. Build the roof trusses using a pattern traced onto the floor as a guide. The triangular soffit support block shown here will provide a nailing surface for the soffit plywood.

Photo 10. Install the 4x4 posts. Make sure they're vertical, then temporarily brace them in both directions. Use a stretch cord to secure the level and keep both hands free for nailing.

Photo 11. Lift the prebuilt beam onto the posts. Use metal post-to-beam brackets to secure the posts firmly to the beam and help prevent any rocking or movement of the structure.

Photo 12. Install roof trusses every 2 ft., nailing them to the 2x4 and 2x6 ribbons and the beam. Use four 16d nails, two toenailed from each side, to make each of the connections.

Photo 13. Sheath and shingle the roof. The metal V-shaped flashing at the peak must fit under the siding and over the roofing felt and shingles to make a weathertight seal.

Finish Your Classic Front Porch

Install the Decorative Features

What really makes this front porch a classic is the attention to detail given in its decorative features. The materials you choose for skirting, ceiling, beams, and railings will create the overall impact you want.

Skirting

You may decide not to add a porch skirt at all. Or you may choose to landscape right up to the porch to cover the open edges. Another option is to attach latticework, available at lumberyards and home centers.

If you do opt for solid skirting, the finished panels should be tall enough to cover the framework of the porch floor, yet short enough to allow air to circulate beneath the porch (Photo 14). It is worth making the skirting panels easily removable, for cleaning and to retrieve toys or other objects that find their way underneath.

▶ Build a skirting frame from 1x4 cedar boards, using corrugated fasteners on the back side to hold the corners together. With a 3/8-inch rabbet router bit, create a recess along the back edge (Photo 14). Then nail a 3/8-inch rough-sawn cedar panel into the recess itself.

Ceiling

▶ Cover your porch ceiling with beaded ceiling board for a classic look, as in this project (Photo 15). Fit warped boards into position by pounding a block of scrap wood against them. Then toenail the bead board into the ceiling crossties with 6d galvanized finish nails.

Posts and Beams

▶ Wrap the posts and beams with knot-free pine for a finished surface (Photo 16). Nail 1x4's along the bottoms of the beams, then cover the sides of the beams with 1x10 or 1x12 sections ripped to width so that they extend 1/8 to 1/4 inch below the 1x4 on the bottom of the beam (see the top right detail of the Construction Plan on page 126).

▶ Fur out one side of each 4x4 post, then secure 1x4's along the sides of each post and 1x6's along the other two faces. Furring out the posts allows you to use standard 1x4 and 1x6 materials when you wrap the posts.

The project shown here makes use of 30-inch tall posts along each side of the stairway. They are secured to the deck with L-brackets, then wrapped and trimmed like full-length posts. The decorative half-width posts installed where the railings meet the house provide a flat surface for the railings and side beams to butt against (see the Construction Plan).

Railings

Building your porch's railings can be a creative activity, as long as you follow the local building codes. Generally, if your porch floor is 30 inches or more off the ground, your railing height must be at least 36 inches. And in most locales the spacing between balusters must be narrow enough so that a 4-inch diameter ball can't pass between them.

Many ornate railings are sold as precut systems in which the shoe and hand rails are grooved to accept the squared-off portion of the balusters and the small filler pieces called fillets (Photo 17). Review these features in the Classic Porch Railing Details (page 136) and refer to them as you proceed.

▶ Use a power miter saw to cut pairs of shoe and hand rails to fit between each set of posts. Be sure to measure and cut carefully. On a scrap piece of 1x2, lay out a long series of balusters and fillets. The porch shown here used 1-5/8 inch balusters with 2-inch fillets. Place this "layout stick" next to your precut shoe and hand rails, then shift the stick left or right until you find a layout that's symmetrical and still leaves equal spaces of 1 to 2 inches between each end baluster and post (Photo 18).

▶ Transfer your layout marks to the pair of shoe and hand rails. Toenail the first baluster to the handrail at the proper distance from the end, then continue adding the precut fillets and balusters (Photo 17). Use two 4d galvanized finish nails to toenail the open side of each baluster to the rail and 1-inch brads to secure each fillet.

▶ Position the shoe rail over the free ends of the balusters after you have installed all the handrail balusters and fillets. Drive a drywall screw through the bottom shoe rail and into the two correctly positioned end balusters. Flip over the railing section and then, starting from one end, nail the balusters and fillets to the shoe rail.

▶ Place support blocks at each end and midway between the shoe rail and the porch floor. Secure each preassembled railing section to the posts with 3-1/2 inch galvanized drywall screws driven at an angle (Photo 18).

Photo 14. Build the skirt frames from cedar 1x4's joined with corrugated fasteners. Use a 3/8-in. rabbeting bit to recess the back side of the frame, then install the plywood panel.

Photo 15. Nail beaded ceiling board to the ceiling crossties. Pound against a scrap block of wood if necessary to force each groove into the tongue of the previous board.

Photo 16. Wrap the posts and beams with stock pine boards. Nail 1x4's to the sides of the posts and 1x6's to their faces using 8d galvanized casing nails.

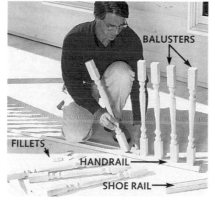

Photo 17. Prebuild the railing sections. First cut pairs of shoe and hand rails to fit between the posts. Then lay out and install the pickets with fillets between each pair.

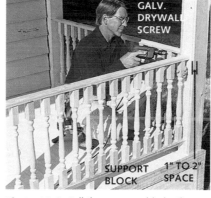

Photo 18. Install the preassembled railing sections between the posts. Use support blocks to hold the sections an equal distance above the deck and provide extra support.

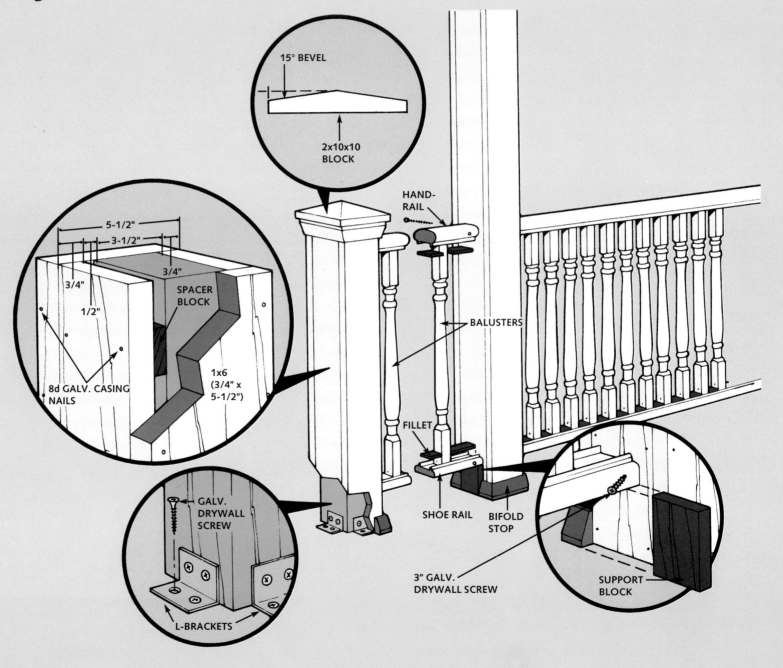

Classic Porch Railing

There is a wide range of precut ornate railing systems that can be installed to give your porch a classic look. Follow the text and photos on pages 134–135 to see how to cut and attach shoe and hand rails to hold the turned balusters.

15° BEVEL

2x10x10 BLOCK

HAND-RAIL

5-1/2"

3-1/2"

3/4"

3/4"

1/2"

SPACER BLOCK

1x6 (3/4" x 5-1/2")

8d GALV. CASING NAILS

BALUSTERS

FILLET

GALV. DRYWALL SCREW

L-BRACKETS

SHOE RAIL

BIFOLD STOP

3" GALV. DRYWALL SCREW

SUPPORT BLOCK

Finishing Touches

To make the most of the time you've spent so far, take just a bit more to enhance what you've created and ensure its long life.

▶ Nail the bifold stop and parting-stop trim pieces around the tops and bottoms of the six freestanding posts and the two half-width posts against the house (see the Construction Plan on page 126 and Classic Porch Railing Details, opposite). Install the trim pieces around the perimeter of the ceiling where it touches the house and beams.

▶ Build stairs or steps as appropriate. This particular porch needed only a simple box stair with tongue-and-groove flooring, faced with the same rough-sawn cedar used for the porch's skirt panels. You may choose not to add risers, but the overall effect will be better if you do.

▶ Fill any gaps with a high-quality paintable caulk. Cover the porch floor—which you should have primed at the point of laying the boards, as suggested—with

two coats of high-quality oil-base paint. Or, for easier application, give the wood a coat of deck enamel thinned with one part solvent to nine parts enamel, then use unthinned enamel for the top coat.

▶ Now protect the rest of the porch's components with a latex primer and two coats of high-quality latex paint. Be meticulous—a thorough paint job will not only make your porch look better but will ensure that it lasts longer.

Attention to detail from top to bottom really pays off whether you can see it (such as the optional stair risers) or not, like the roofing felt or polyethylene film tucked under the flashing behind the siding.

Rambler Front Porch

Before the age of electronic entertainment, a home's front porch was its social center—

a place to knit while keeping an eye on the kids in the yard, to gather and watch

a storm brew on a hot summer night, or just to sit and chat.

Front porches aren't only for rural farmhouses. They look great, and work

just as well, on suburban one-story ramblers, too. Building a front porch like this

one may well be the most rewarding project you've done for a long time.

A front porch needn't be complex or elaborate to work its welcoming magic on the front of your home.

Construction Plans

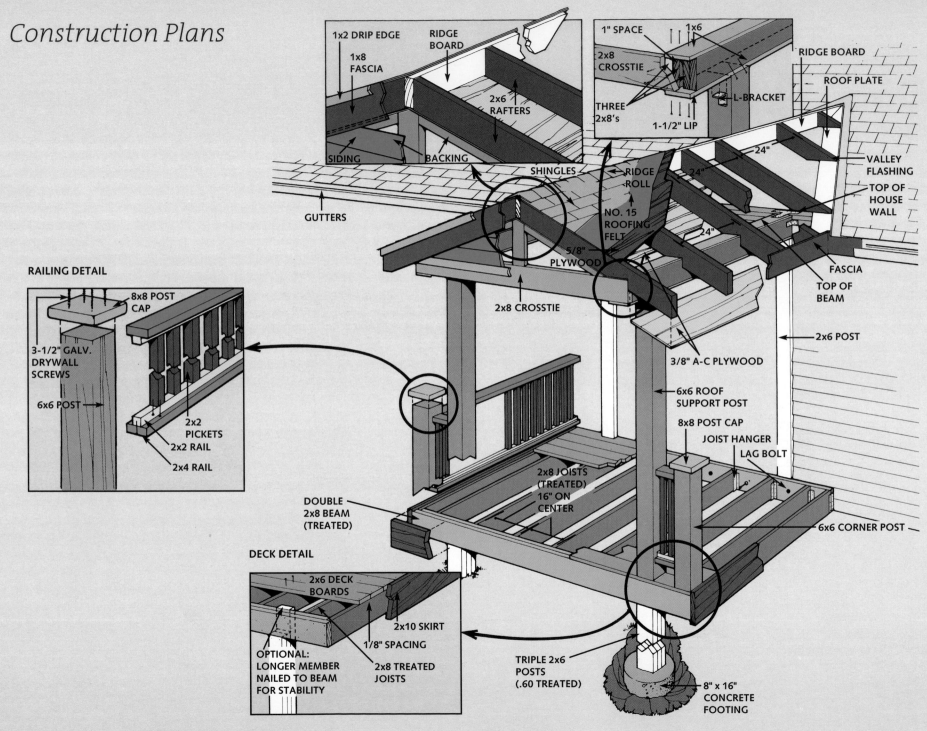

1x2 DRIP EDGE

RIDGE BOARD

1x8 FASCIA

2x6 RAFTERS

SIDING

BACKING

SHINGLES

GUTTERS

1" SPACE

1x6

2x8 CROSSTIE

L-BRACKET

THREE 2x8's

1-1/2" LIP

RIDGE BOARD

ROOF PLATE

24"

24"

24"

VALLEY FLASHING

TOP OF HOUSE WALL

FASCIA

TOP OF BEAM

2x6 POST

RIDGE ROLL

NO. 15 ROOFING FELT

5/8" PLYWOOD

2x8 CROSSTIE

3/8" A-C PLYWOOD

6x6 ROOF SUPPORT POST

8x8 POST CAP

JOIST HANGER

LAG BOLT

RAILING DETAIL

8x8 POST CAP

3-1/2" GALV. DRYWALL SCREWS

6x6 POST

2x2 PICKETS

2x2 RAIL

2x4 RAIL

DOUBLE 2x8 BEAM (TREATED)

2x8 JOISTS (TREATED) 16" ON CENTER

6x6 CORNER POST

DECK DETAIL

2x6 DECK BOARDS

2x10 SKIRT

1/8" SPACING

2x8 TREATED JOISTS

OPTIONAL: LONGER MEMBER NAILED TO BEAM FOR STABILITY

TRIPLE 2x6 POSTS (.60 TREATED)

8" x 16" CONCRETE FOOTING

Plan Your Rambler Front Porch

This project requires careful planning, because of the need to fit this porch's roof into the roof of your house. And because this porch uses front-yard footage, it is important to make sure your design is approved by a building inspector before you begin, as discussed on the next page.

Skill and Time Considerations

If you've ever built an outdoor deck, you already know how to construct the bottom half of this project, the easiest part. However, this porch becomes more complicated as you get to the roof and eaves. Achieving a leakproof structure that looks like an integral part of your home requires careful planning and skilled carpentry. You should figure on its taking two reasonably experienced do-it-yourselfers most of their spare time for a month to complete this project.

Because this is not a project for beginners, these instructions don't attempt to provide specific angle measurements and materials specifications. You will need to adapt this design to suit your own house. For instance, the roof pitch, eave length, and window placement here are probably different from those of your home.

If this porch project appears to be beyond your skills, consider building only part of it yourself. Think about hiring an architect or designer for at least the design-approval stage if you need help. And hire a qualified contractor to erect the porch deck, posts, and roof. Once the skeleton is assembled, you can complete the railings, steps, and siding, then apply the finish yourself.

Cost Factors

When budgeting for a porch project of this size (approximately 6x10 feet), consider more than just the cost of the lumber, siding, and shingles. You will also have outlays for paint, stain, gutters, and a new light fixture. And you may also need to liven up or add to your existing landscaping. For a close cost estimate, take your final plans to a full-service lumberyard and a nursery for review.

Materials

Four types of lumber were used to build this porch, to achieve a good balance between longevity and cost effectiveness.

▶ Pressure-treated 2x6 deck-support posts stamped .60 (60-pound) for below-grade (underground) use.

▶ Pressure-treated 2x8 deck joists, deck beams, and ledger boards rated .40 (40-pound) for aboveground use.

▶ Rot-resistant cedar for the porch floor, roof-support posts, siding, and railings. (Redwood and pressure-treated .40 lumber would also work well.)

▶ Pine lumber and common plywood for the roof beams, rafters, and sheathing. Prime and paint these exposed materials to prevent rot.

Design Considerations

It's much easier to build a porch that blends in seamlessly with a house when they're both designed and built at the same time. That's why porches added after a house has been built often appear tacked on. And small, single-story ranch homes like the one shown here present their own special challenge: They're often unadorned and small, with windows that crowd the front door.

This particular porch design managed to solve all of these problems. Whether you copy it exactly, adapt parts of it, or start from scratch to design a different porch altogether, here are some basic design considerations.

▶ Plan a sitting porch to extend at least 4 to 6 feet from the house and a minimum of 6 to 8 feet wide. To keep it in proportion to the house, let it span no more than one-quarter to one-third of the house's width.

▶ Design your porch to look and feel as solid and permanent as the house itself. Don't skimp when you build the floor and stairs or size the columns and corner posts.

Tools You Need

Hand Tools

Carpenter's level

Face mask, goggles

Framing square

Hammer

Posthole digger

Pry bar

Sledgehammer

String lines, batter boards

Utility knife with shingle-cutting blade

Power Tools

Circular saw

Reciprocal saw

Optional

8-in. auger

▶ Blend your porch into the rest of your home by using the same paint colors, shingles, siding, and trim.

▶ Set the porch a few steps off the ground, if possible, for improved ventilation and a better view.

▶ Personalize your porch with a unique railing or unusual light fixture. Include places to hang wind chimes, mobiles, plants, weather gauges, or whatever you like.

▶ Consider including a place to set down packages and groceries while you search for your keys. It could be something as simple as a built-in bench or as elaborate as a porch swing.

Building-Code Considerations

Sometimes, obtaining permission to build the front porch of your dreams may seem more difficult than the actual building of it. One point to settle that comes up regularly is the height of railings and the spacing between balusters. But the main issue for this project is local setback restrictions, which will dictate how close the front of your house or porch can come to your front property line. Typical front setbacks are 30 to 40 feet from the property line, which is not necessarily the same point as the curb. Many municipalities impose an additional 10- to 15-foot right-of-way between the curb and your property line.

Many suburban homes were built with their front doors right on the setback line. This practice resulted in communities that were uniform from block to block and made possible the biggest backyards, but it didn't always allow space to add a front porch.

Therefore, the first step in planning your deck should be to check with your local building inspector. Keep these points in mind.

▶ To obtain a building permit, you must present a survey showing the exact position of your home on your lot and that of the proposed addition in relation to the setback and property lines. Your municipal office can probably provide you inexpensively with a copy of your lot survey.

▶ If your planned porch does in fact protrude into the setback area, you can apply for a variance, or exception for your porch. This process often involves a series of hearings, which may take weeks and can cost several hundred dollars.

▶ You'll increase your chances of being granted a variance if you can present an attractive, well-thought-out design, especially one professionally prepared by an architect. Many cities have come to view porches as community builders and now encourage homeowners to add them, because often if just one or two homeowners construct porches this is enough to spark similar interest on the block.

▶ During the energy crisis of the 1970s, many cities changed their zoning regulations to allow enclosed entry vestibules (called air-lock entries) to extend beyond the setback boundaries and allowed porches to be included at their sides. It might be worth finding out if this was done where you live.

Construct Your Rambler Front Porch

Remove the Old Stoop

Before you can build your new porch, you first may have to demolish stairs, a stoop, or an old porch. If there's a full step down to the stoop, you may be able to leave the old one in place and build the framework of the new porch around it. For specifics on how to do this, see the previous chapter (page 130). However, in many cases the front stoop will be nearly door threshold height and need to be removed (Photo 1).

Be aware that many concrete stoops on houses more than forty years old are over an old well or well room. A glass block in the center of the stoop that serves as an access panel to remove the pump for repairs is a clue that you may have such a well. If so, consult your building inspector.

In most cases, only the outer 2 to 6 inches will be solid concrete; the rest is usually fill material like dirt, sand, and building debris.
▶ Start at a corner or edge breaking up the concrete with a sledgehammer and work toward the center. Wear appropriate face and eye protection (see box at right).
▶ Use scrap sheets of paneling to protect adjacent surfaces of your house (Photo 2).

For specifics on how to do this, see the previous chapter (page 130).

TECHNIQUES
Demolition Protection

Breaking up concrete or stone results in flying chips and large chunks of debris that can be dangerous to anyone facing the demolition work. Make sure that you and anyone helping or observing have proper eye and face protection.

Don't rely on ordinary eyeglasses to shield your eyes—they can even cause serious injury if debris shatters them. Wear special protective safety glasses with side shields or safety goggles, which can be worn over regular eyeglasses. For demolition of the sort described here, goggles with direct vents through the side pieces provide air circulation as well as protection. Keep your goggles clear with a bottle of window cleaner and a roll of paper towels.

For full-face protection, wear a face shield with a chin guard, or perhaps a full-face wire mesh guard. To keep your plastic face shield clean and scratch-free, cover its front with clear plastic wrap. This won't affect your vision, and when it gets dirty you can just peel it off and replace it.

REMOVE THE OLD STOOP

Photo 1. Because this stoop lacked the necessary full step down from the front door, there was not enough room to leave it and frame the new porch around it.

SCRAP WOOD TO PROTECT HOUSE AND DOOR

SAFETY GLASSES

Photo 2. Demolish and remove the old concrete stoop or slab. Most stoops aren't solid but are filled with dirt, loose building debris, and scrap concrete.

Build the Porch Deck

Once the site has been cleared, lay out the perimeter of your new porch, identify the footing locations, pour the footings, and install the base posts. For a more detailed description of these steps, see "Deck Builder's Companion" (pages 12–21).

Installing the Footings and Posts

The footing support and roof posts for this porch were set 1 foot in from the corners. Doing so created a larger floor area and avoided obstructing the windows beside the door.

▶ Establish the perimeter of your porch with string lines and batter boards. The batter boards allow you to move and fine-tune the locations of the strings to establish a square floor. They are easily made by trimming the ends of 2x2's to a point with a circular saw, then screwing on 1x4 crosspieces 2 inches or so below the tops of the stakes. Once you have placed your batter boards, check for squareness by measuring the diagonals (Photo 3).

▶ Next, dig holes for the 8x16 concrete footing pads and deck-support posts (see the Construction Plan on page 140), to at least 6 inches below frost line. Consult your building inspector to find out where the frost line is in your area and what the recommended dimensions are for your footings. Make sure the footing holes are wider at the bottom than the top, to protect against frost heaves.

▶ Fill the footing holes with enough concrete to make solid pads for the base posts (Photo 4).

▶ Attach the ledger board to the house's framework, using lag bolts every 2 feet. To attach the ledger board to concrete, use heavy-duty masonry anchors. (For more on how to attach a ledger board to framing, see "Showcase Deck," pages 26–27; for tips on securing ledger boards to concrete, see "Deck Builder's Companion," page 18.)

▶ Secure joist hangers to the ledger board every 16 inches with joist-hanger nails.

▶ Use a straight board and a level to establish the correct height for one member of the deck posts, level with the bottoms of the joist hangers (Photo 5).

▶ Cut three treated 2x6's to length for each post, nail them together, then reposition this triple support post on the concrete footing pad. Repeat for the other post.

Installing the Joists and Decking

▶ Rest a doubled, pressure-treated 2x8 beam across the two deck posts.

▶ Add joist hangers spaced at 16-inch intervals.

▶ Cut and install the treated 2x8 joists (Photo 6). Sight along the joists before you nail them in place, to make sure the crowned, or curved, edges are upward.

Now your deck's perimeter should mirror the original outline established by the strings and batter boards.

▶ Finish the decking by nailing 2x6 cedar decking to the joists using 16d galvanized nails for both spacing and securing the boards (Photo 7).

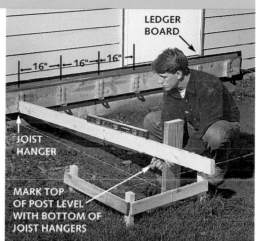

Photo 3. Establish the perimeter of the porch using batter boards and string. Check for squareness by measuring across the corners.

Photo 4. Shovel concrete into the bottoms of holes dug to 6 in. below frost line. These concrete pads will provide solid bases for the support posts.

Photo 5. Mark the tops of the post members level with the bottoms of the joist hangers. Place triple 2x6 posts on the concrete pads in the footing holes.

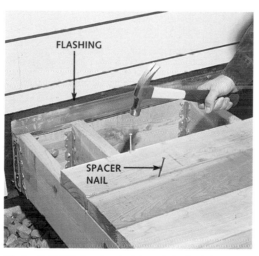

Photo 6. Install a treated 2x8 double front beam, then the joist hangers, spaced 16 in. apart. Nail in the joists, making sure the floor remains square.

Photo 7. Nail 2x6 cedar deck boards to the joists, using 16d galvanized common nails as both fasteners and spacers between the boards as shown.

Build the Roof

Constructing the roof is the most challenging part of this porch project. After reviewing the photos, illustrations, and text, if you feel uncertain about your abilities to complete this stage properly, consult books on basic carpentry framing or consider hiring a professional for this part of the job.

Attaching the Supports and Beams

▶ With a level, draw vertical lines up the side of the house to mark the positions of the roof-support posts. In this case, the position is 12 inches in from the edges of the deck, as explained on page 144.

▶ Remove the siding between these lines, using a circular saw.

▶ Next, remove the soffit plywood or boards covering the underside of the eave.

▶ Saw through and remove all exposed rafter tails, fascia boards, roof sheathing,

and shingles that fall between these marked lines, back to the face of the house (Photo 8).

Rent or borrow a reciprocating saw to make the soffit and eave cuts.

It can be difficult to determine exactly where to cut off the gutters and fascia and soffit boards. Instead of guessing, remove more of these components than seems necessary, all the way back to the next joint or full board, even if it's as far as 10 feet away. This added leeway will make it easier to blend the old construction with the new when you reinstall these pieces.

▶ Now cut, plumb, and brace the two 6x6 roof-support posts so that they're directly over the treated deck posts.

▶ Bolt the two 2x6 support posts to the framework of the house (Photo 9). Calculate their height so that when the 8-3/4 inch built-up beams rest on them the tops of the

beams will be level with the top of the house wall (see the Construction Plans on page 140). Cut the 6x6 support posts to the same height.

▶ Build up the roof beams from 2x8's and 1x6's (see the Beam Details, top right, on page 140). Make the beams long enough to provide a 16-inch overhang (Photo 10).

▶ Lift the beams into place and secure them to the house and support posts with 16d galvanized nails and metal L-brackets.

▶ Finally, firmly nail the 2x8 roof crosstie across the ends of the two beams to provide additional support.

Installing the Rafters and Ridge Board

Experienced carpenters determine the length and angles of roof rafters by using a framing square, which has inscribed a rafter table that gives the length per foot of run for a variety of common rafters. But you can also compute the dimension or arrive at it by drawing a full-size replica (see the diagram on the facing page). To make a rafter full-size template, proceed as follows, referring to the drawing at right.

▶ Connect both pairs of 2x6 and 6x6 support posts with lines drawn lightly on the porch floor to represent the beam above. Draw a pair of lines 1-1/2 inches apart midway between them to represent the ridge board.

▶ Lay a 2x6 at an angle across the ridge board lines and beam lines drawn on the floor. Adjust the angle of the 2x6 to the slope you want for your porch roof. This porch has a moderate 6/12 roof, meaning that it rises 6 inches vertically for every 12 inches of horizontal run. Using a large

BUILD THE ROOF: ATTACHING THE SUPPORTS AND BEAMS

Photo 8. Remove the portion of the house eave that juts into the porch area. Work from both above and below to remove the roof in chunks.

Photo 9. Plumb and brace the two 6x6 roof-support posts directly over the treated deck posts. Remove the siding, then fasten two 2x6 supports to the house front.

Photo 10. Assemble the roof beams, then lift them onto the posts. Secure them to the posts and house with 16d galvanized nails and metal L-brackets.

protractor, speed square, or framing square as a guide, cut one end of the rafter so that it butts against the ridge-board line drawn on the floor.

▶ Mark where this rafter intersects each side of the beam lines on the floor. Connect these marks to create the bird's-mouth, or seat cut, where the rafter rests on the beam.

▶ Cut a pair of rafters from this pattern and tack them together with a 2x4 block between to represent the ridge board. Position this "flying V" on top of the beams in line with the house's rafter tails.

▶ Mark the uncut ends of the porch rafters where they intersect the rafter tails on the house, then take the rafters down. Cut the porch tails to length at the same angle as the rafters' ridge cut.

▶ Now cut the remaining rafters, using these pieces as patterns.

▶ To determine the length of the ridge board, angle-cut one end of a long 2x6 to match your home's roof slope (Photo 11).

Photo 11. Nail the rafters to the ridge board and beams. One end of the ridge board is cut to the roof slope, the other even with the outside rafters.

Tack two precut rafters on the outer ends of the beams above the crosstie. With a helper, place the ridge board between these rafters while moving the angle-cut end of the ridge board up and down the house roof to level the ridge board. Check that the two end rafters are vertically aligned with the 2x8 roof crosstie below. Then tack the ridge board to the rafters and house roof. Check

once again to make sure everything is level, plumb, and centered.

▶ Mark the ridge board where the rafters attach, take it down, and cut it to length. Then reposition the ridge board and install rafters every 24 inches, toenailing them to the ridge board and beams. Insert the last full-length rafters so their tails meet either the tails of the house rafters or the line they create.

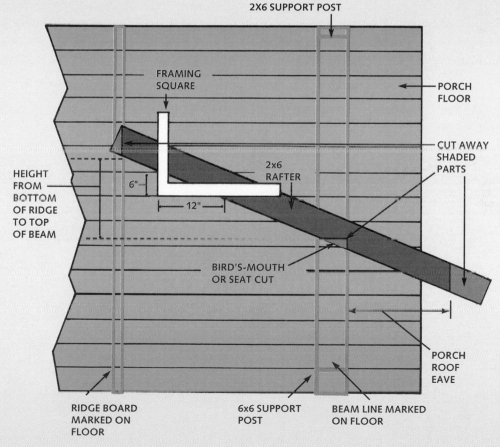

DIAGRAM

Rafter Template Plan

2X6 SUPPORT POST

FRAMING SQUARE

PORCH FLOOR

HEIGHT FROM BOTTOM OF RIDGE TO TOP OF BEAM

6"

12"

2x6 RAFTER

CUT AWAY SHADED PARTS

BIRD'S-MOUTH OR SEAT CUT

PORCH ROOF EAVE

RIDGE BOARD MARKED ON FLOOR

6x6 SUPPORT POST

BEAM LINE MARKED ON FLOOR

2x6 RIDGE BOARD

2x6 RAFTERS

2x8 ROOF CROSSTIE

Adding the Sheathing

▶ Nail a 2x6 roof plate between the end of the ridge board and the last full-length rafter installed on each side.

▶ Cut and fit shorter jack rafters between the ridge board and the roof plates, positioning them every 24 inches. The cuts at the ridge board will be the same as those on all of the full-length rafters, but the cuts at the roof plates involve cutting a tricky compound angle to match the slope of the house roof (see "Making Compound Cuts," page 164, and Photo 12).

▶ Measure, cut, and secure 5/8-inch plywood sheathing to the porch rafters with 8d nails (Photo 13).

▶ Use a utility knife with a shingle-cutting blade to cut back and remove a 2-inch strip of shingles from the house roof in the valley where the porch roof adjoins. Use a pry bar to pull up the fragile shingles gently. Tuck No. 15 roofing felt, or a polyethylene film, then galvanized valley flashing 8 inches up under the shingles and onto the old roof, pulling up existing roofing nails where necessary (Photo 14).

▶ Finally, shingle the porch roof, following the manufacturer's directions supplied with the shingles.

BUILD THE ROOF: ADDING THE SHEATHING

COMPOUND ANGLES

SAW BASE TILTED TO MATCH SLOPE OF ROOF

PLYWOOD CUT EVEN WITH RAFTER

SHORTENED JACK RAFTERS

ROOF PLATE

VALLEY FLASHING

UTILITY KNIFE WITH SHINGLE-CUTTING BLADE

ROOFING FELT AND FLASHING TUCKED 8" BENEATH SHINGLES

Photo 12. Install short jack rafters every 24 in. where the porch meets the house. The ends that join the roof are cut at a difficult compound angle.

Photo 13. Nail roof sheathing to the rafters with 8d nails. The roof plate helps distribute the weight of the jack rafters evenly over a larger area.

Photo 14. Shingle the roof by tucking No. 15 roofing felt or polyethylene film, then galvanized metal flashing, 8 in. under the shingles on the existing roof.

Complete the Porch

The final steps are to make a smooth joint between the new and old roofs, add siding and skirting, and construct railings.

Enclosing the Roof

▶ Use 2x4 backing studs and plywood sheathing to create a flat surface where the new porch roof intersects the front of the house wall (Photo 15). If you have any old insulation on hand, you might want to use it to supplement what's exposed while this area is accessible.

▶ Now measure, cut, and install sheets of 1/2-inch A-C exterior-grade (G1S or Select in Canada) plywood to the bottoms of the rafters to make a soffit ceiling on both sides of the roof support beams (Photo 16).

▶ Where the porch eaves and house eaves intersect, cut cardboard templates to help you determine the exact angles and widths to cut the exterior soffits (Photo 17). Then trace these templates onto the A-C exterior-grade plywood to be used for the soffits.

Photo 15. Nail plywood sheathing over 2x4 backing studs to create a flat surface where the new roof intersects the front of the house wall.

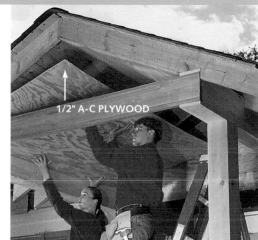

Photo 16. Measure, cut, and fit a smooth 1/2-in. A-C exterior-grade plywood soffit to the underside of the rafters on each side of the ridge board.

Photo 17. Use cardboard templates to determine the exact width and angle of the exterior soffits where the eaves intersect.

Adding Siding and Skirting

▶ Install tongue-and-groove cedar siding between the 2x6 support posts, using a wood block to protect the siding's tongues as you tap the boards in place (Photo 18).

▶ Add 1x8 fascia boards to the rafter tails and gable ends.

▶ Close the gable end, then nail lap siding to the backer blocks (Photo 19) and A-C exterior-grade (G1S or Select in Canada) plywood to the back side.

▶ Install gutters to the new porch's eaves. If necessary, adjust the slope of the gutters on the house where the two join.

▶ Measure, cut, and nail decorative 2x10 cedar skirting around the perimeter of the deck, covering the cut ends of the deck boards and deck framework.

Lap Siding

Even though lap siding tends to be more expensive than shingles or aluminum and vinyl siding, for example, it can have a life span of 30 years or more.

COMPLETE THE PORCH: ADDING SIDING AND SKIRTING

Photo 18. Nail the siding in place. Use a scrap piece of wood to protect the tongue of the new siding as you tap it into place.

Photo 19. Nail lap siding to backer blocks at the gable end. Cover the back side of the gable end with smooth A-C exterior-grade plywood.

Build the Railings

Take the time to design and plan railings and handrails for your porch that will add personality and character. You can use ordinary lumber or more elaborate round spindles. If the floor of your porch is at least 30 inches off the ground, your railing must be a minimum of 36 inches high and the pickets less than 4 inches apart. Check with your local building inspector for additional railing and handrail requirements. More information on upper and lower deck railings is available in "Deck Builder's Companion" (pages 12–21). Refer also to the Railing Detail on page 140.

▶ To build the railings shown here, start by constructing two 6x6 cedar posts at the outside corners and build the railing in modular sections.

▶ Mark the spacing for 2x2 cedar pickets on pairs of 2x2 cedar rails (Photo 20). Measure and cut the pickets, then nail them between the rails.

▶ Add 2x4 cedar top and bottom rails and attach the sections to the house and posts (Photo 21). Use spacer blocks to hold the sections 4 inches off the porch floor while you attach them.

▶ Finally, screw 8x8 cedar post caps on top of the corner posts to protect the posts' vulnerable end grain from moisture.

Finishing Touches

Once you add stairs and a finish to the new surfaces, you're ready to sit and rock on your new porch and get reacquainted with the old neighborhood.

Stairs

The stairs shown here are simply two boxes stacked on top of each other and then fastened to the deck support posts. When planning your stairs, make them as wide as possible. Wide stairs are safer and also provide space for flowerpots and decorations. More information on stair construction is available in "Backyard Island" (pages 56–57).

For added safety on stairs, paint them with a mixture of 1 part clean white fine sand to 4 parts paint. Or glue down nonslip tread strips with an exterior adhesive.

Finishes

▶ For longevity, use a high-quality stain on the porch floor. Stain penetrates wood better than paint, is less likely to flake, and is easier to touch up.

▶ Use paint or stain to finish the rest of the porch to match the exterior of your house. Add appropriate landscaping to make your new porch seem even more like a natural extension of your house.

It is best to wait a few months before painting pressure-treated wood unless it is marked KDAT (kiln dried after treatment). The pressure-treating process saturates the wood with chemicals, usually leaving it too wet to accept paint or stain well initially.

BUILD THE RAILINGS

RAILING CORNER POST

2x2 HORIZONTAL RAILS (2" SPACING)

← 2x10 SKIRT

Photo 20. Secure 2x2 pickets to 2x2 rails with 8d galvanized casing nails, then nail 2x4 rails along the top and bottom.

2x2 PICKETS

2x4 HORIZONTAL RAILS

SPACER BLOCKS

Photo 21. Install the preassembled railing sections between the 6x6 posts and the siding. Use spacer blocks to position the railing 4 in. off the porch floor.

Open-Air Gazebo

Can you remember the first gazebo you saw as a child?

You may have marveled at how the lacy wood structure climbed gracefully

up from eight posts to a single point at the peak of the roof.

And it allowed you to look out in any direction.

This gazebo has eight sides, just like the classics of old, but don't let all the angles scare you.

If you own basic carpentry tools and have some deck-building experience,

you can successfully tackle this project.

Building this gazebo does more than provide a protected spot to dine, relax, and enjoy the outdoors in your yard. It also adds a touch of nostalgia and romance you won't find with any other outdoor structure.

Construction Plan

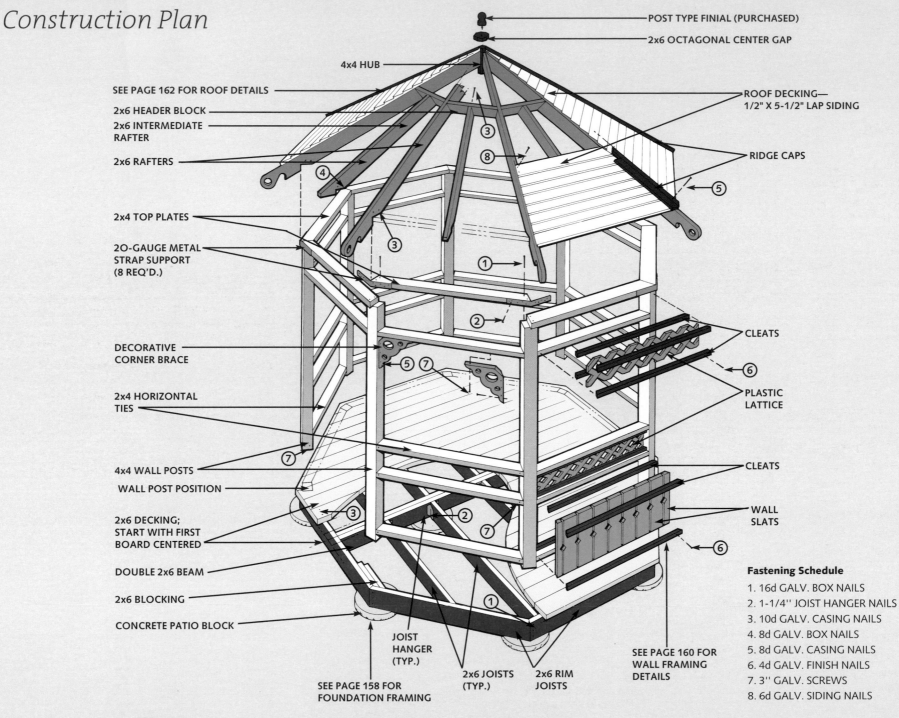

POST TYPE FINIAL (PURCHASED)

2x6 OCTAGONAL CENTER GAP

4x4 HUB

SEE PAGE 162 FOR ROOF DETAILS

2x6 HEADER BLOCK

2x6 INTERMEDIATE RAFTER

2x6 RAFTERS

2x4 TOP PLATES

20-GAUGE METAL STRAP SUPPORT (8 REQ'D.)

DECORATIVE CORNER BRACE

2x4 HORIZONTAL TIES

4x4 WALL POSTS

WALL POST POSITION

2x6 DECKING; START WITH FIRST BOARD CENTERED

DOUBLE 2x6 BEAM

2x6 BLOCKING

CONCRETE PATIO BLOCK

ROOF DECKING— 1/2" X 5-1/2" LAP SIDING

RIDGE CAPS

CLEATS

PLASTIC LATTICE

CLEATS

WALL SLATS

JOIST HANGER (TYP.)

2x6 JOISTS (TYP.)

2x6 RIM JOISTS

SEE PAGE 158 FOR FOUNDATION FRAMING

SEE PAGE 160 FOR WALL FRAMING DETAILS

Fastening Schedule

1. 16d GALV. BOX NAILS
2. 1-1/4'' JOIST HANGER NAILS
3. 10d GALV. CASING NAILS
4. 8d GALV. BOX NAILS
5. 8d GALV. CASING NAILS
6. 4d GALV. FINISH NAILS
7. 3'' GALV. SCREWS
8. 6d GALV. SIDING NAILS

Plan Your Gazebo

Preliminary Considerations

Unlike many of the other projects in this book, this gazebo is freestanding rather than attached to the house. Therefore, some of the normal building-code regulations do not apply; footings can be shallower, or you can even use patio blocks in their place if the surface soil is stable enough. In northern climates you will need to pour footings that can withstand the ground heaving that would throw the whole construction askew if it were set on patio blocks. For more information on pouring, see pages 16–17. You would still be wise, however, to show your completed plans to a local building inspector. Enlisting that professional's advice may help you define your project and buy materials most economically.

Because you will no doubt want to adapt these plans to fit your own site, the measurements supplied here should be taken simply as guides. A full shopping list of materials will need to be prepared with your own specifications in mind. You will in any event need galvanized box and casing nails in sizes from 4d to 16d, and galvanized screws, as described in the Fastening Schedule on the facing page. And it is best to use a long-lasting wood like cedar for such key elements of the design as the decking, bracing, posts, rails, and roof siding. The deck's framing should employ .40 pressure-treated 2x6's.

Tool and Time Factors

To build this gazebo you'll need only the standard hand tools like hammers and saws and measuring aids, as well as basic power tools you probably own already. If you don't have the power items in the list to the right, they can be rented if not borrowed.

Plan on devoting a full week to building the basic structure. Then you can add the finishing touches over a few weekends.

It's easiest to think of the building process as consisting of five separate steps, each of which will take at least a full eight-hour day to complete.

▶ Build the foundation, using 12-inch round patio blocks stacked and mortared together to form a level surface.
▶ Build the deck with joists and decking.
▶ Prestain or paint the rafters, wall slats, and roof caps.
▶ Assemble the walls and roof.
▶ Cut and install the wall slats, cleats, and lattice sections.

Site Factors

You'll need a relatively flat spot to build this gazebo. The site shown for this project had a slope of 3 inches in 10 feet, which required building up the foundation on the low sides. If you have more than an 8-inch slope in 10 feet, consider choosing a different site or making modifications to your landscaping before you build.

Another alternative is to pour concrete footings rather than using the simpler patio blocks shown here. For full information on how to design and pour proper footings, see Build a Solid Foundation, page 16.

Tools You Need

Hand Tools

Chalk line
4-ft. level
Hammer
Handsaw
Measuring tape
Miter box
Protractor-style cutting guide
Shovel
Stake and mason's cord
Two 8-ft. stepladders

Power Tools

Circular saw
Cordless or electric drill
Jigsaw
1-1/2 and 3-in. hole saws

Construct Your Gazebo

Build the Foundation

The ultimate success of any structure starts with a good foundation. Don't rush this part of the project. For instance, allow at least a full day for the patio-block mortar to set, and at least that time for poured footings to cure, before you start the actual building.

This foundation is nothing more than round patio blocks, 12 inches in diameter, set level with each other and located at ten key points. Plan on having to stack and mortar some of the patio blocks to create a perfectly level foundation. Here's how to locate and level patio blocks.

▶ Scribe a circle with a 65-inch radius on the grass, using mason's cord and a landscaping spike or stake as the center pivot. Keep the string pulled tightly out from the stake as you scribe the circle. This circle will run through the center of each of the ten patio blocks laid out around the perimeter.

▶ Keep the location of the gazebo's entry in mind as you position the foundation blocks. First align a block at one side of the entry.

Then position the next block directly across the circle from this one, using a string line that runs through the center of the circle (Photo 1).

▶ Remove the sod from under each patio block for a firm foundation. Start with the block at the highest elevation and level all of the other blocks to it, using a long, straight 2x6 with a level on top of it (Photo 2). Keep in mind that each mortar joint in a stack of blocks will add 3/8 inch to the final height.

BUILD THE FOUNDATION

ALIGN OPPOSITE PATIO BLOCKS WITH CENTER

LAYOUT CIRCLE

DOORWAY

CIRCULAR PATIO BLOCKS

STRAIGHT 2x6

4' LEVEL

STACKED PATIO BLOCKS

Photo 1. Align the first patio block on one side of the entry. Then set the opposite block, using the center of the layout circle as a guide.

Photo 2. Level the patio blocks so they're all at the same height. To raise low spots, mortar together stacks of blocks, allowing about 3/8 in. for the joints.

Frame the Deck

Framing the deck of this gazebo is actually easier than it might first appear.

▶ First, build the I-shaped beam assembly from treated 2x6's nailed together with two outside rim joists at the ends (Photo 3).

▶ Now position this beam assembly over the two center foundation blocks. Then nail the rest of the joists, including the outer rim joists, to the assembly (Photo 4). Nail the rim joists together, using three 16d galvanized box nails (see the Construction Plan and Fastening Schedule on page 154 and the Foundation and Decking Framing Diagram on page 158). Then add the joist hangers and 2x6 joists.

▶ Next, check the deck framing for level. Adjust the framing members or add shims as necessary before you proceed. If you do need to add any shims, use scrap pieces of treated wood.

▶ Nail in the 2x6 blocking at the four points of the I-shaped beam assembly indicated on the Foundation and Decking Framing Diagram. You'll need the blocking later to support the posts.

▶ Make sure that all the diagonal measurements are equal. If they're not, you may be able to coax the frame into alignment now with a few hammer blows to the corners.

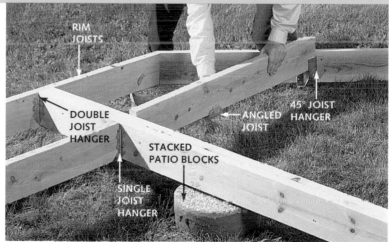

FRAME THE DECK

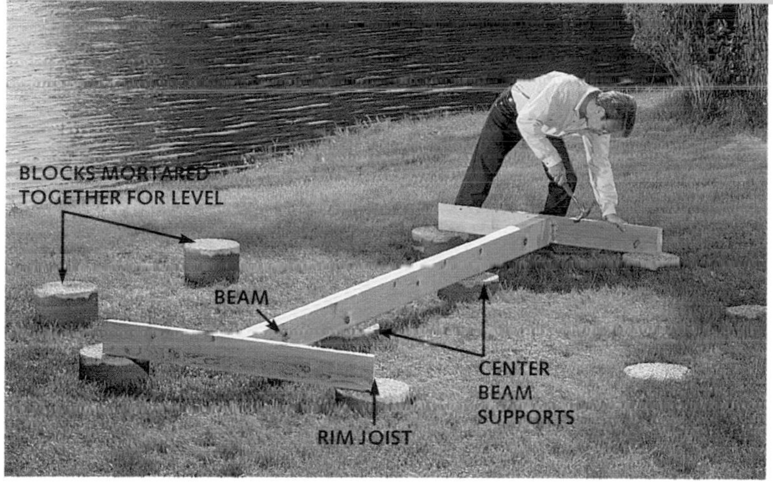

BLOCKS MORTARED TOGETHER FOR LEVEL

BEAM

CENTER BEAM SUPPORTS

RIM JOIST

RIM JOISTS

DOUBLE JOIST HANGER

ANGLED JOIST

45° JOIST HANGER

STACKED PATIO BLOCKS

SINGLE JOIST HANGER

Photo 3. Position the I-shaped beam assembly on the two center patio-block supports. Then nail on the remaining rim joists with 16d galvanized box nails.

Photo 4. Install intermediate joists inside the outer rim. Make sure the diagonal measurements are equal. Use single and double joist hangers for support.

Foundation and Decking Framing

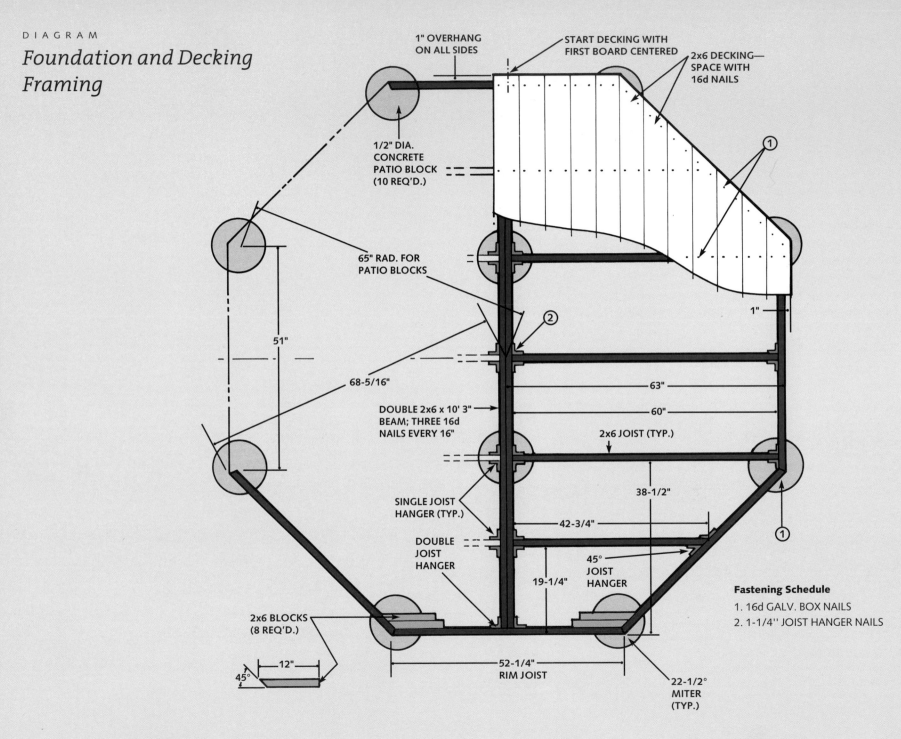

1" OVERHANG ON ALL SIDES

START DECKING WITH FIRST BOARD CENTERED

2x6 DECKING— SPACE WITH 16d NAILS

1/2" DIA. CONCRETE PATIO BLOCK (10 REQ'D.)

①

65" RAD. FOR PATIO BLOCKS

②

1"

51"

68-5/16"

63"

60"

DOUBLE 2x6 x 10' 3" BEAM; THREE 16d NAILS EVERY 16"

2x6 JOIST (TYP.)

38-1/2"

SINGLE JOIST HANGER (TYP.)

42-3/4"

DOUBLE JOIST HANGER

45° JOIST HANGER

19-1/4"

①

Fastening Schedule

1. 16d GALV. BOX NAILS
2. 1-1/4'' JOIST HANGER NAILS

2x6 BLOCKS (8 REQ'D.)

52-1/4" RIM JOIST

22-1/2° MITER (TYP.)

12"

45°

Lay the Decking

Once you are satisfied that the frame is true, proceed building upward, moving from the deck to the walls.

▶ Nail down the 2x6 cedar decking with 16d galvanized finish nails (Photo 5). Start at the center and work outward. You can also use 16d nails as spacers to achieve even 1/8-inch gaps between the boards.

▶ Nail the ends of any bowed boards down before you do their centers. Place the bowed part facing the previous row. Then after nailing down the ends, insert a wide wooden shim to space the boards correctly, and nail the deck boards in their centers.

▶ Make neat joints at board ends by using a miter box to cut clean, square ends. Then butt these ends together over the very center of their shared joist.

▶ Start in the middle with 12-foot boards and work your way to each end, using first 10-foot and then 8-foot stock. Be sure the decking is perpendicular to the joists.

▶ Let the deck boards extend over the rim joists as you nail them down. Then, when all the decking is in place, snap a chalk line 1 inch beyond the rim joists and cut the boards along it (Photo 6).

LAY THE DECKING

2x6 DECKING

JOISTS

DOORWAY

Photo 5. Nail the 2x6 cedar decking to the joists with 16d galvanized finish nails. Start in the middle and work your way out.

LEAVE 1" FOR OVERHANG

CHALK LINE

Photo 6. Snap a chalk line 1 in. beyond the outside of the rim joists as a cutting guide. Then trim the decking along it with a circular saw.

Wall Framing Details

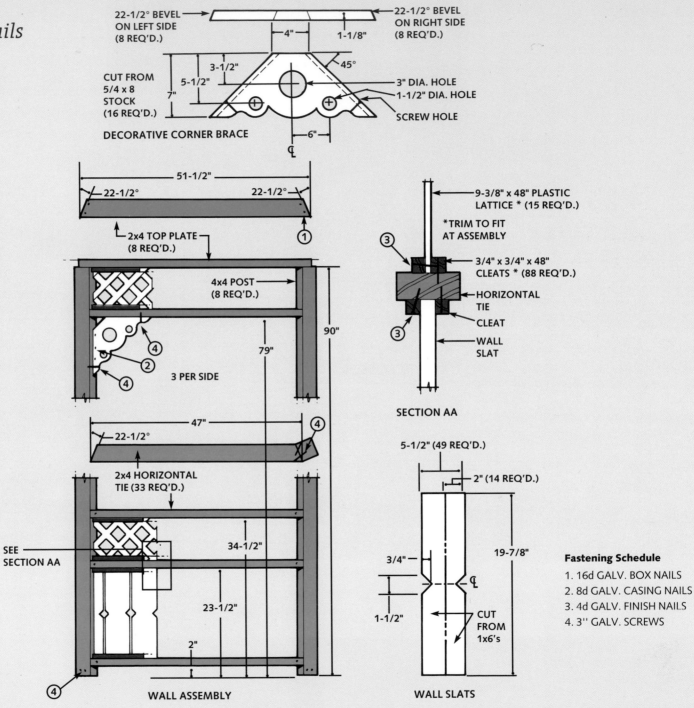

22-1/2° BEVEL
ON LEFT SIDE
(8 REQ'D.)

22-1/2° BEVEL
ON RIGHT SIDE
(8 REQ'D.)

4"

1-1/8"

3-1/2"

5-1/2"

7"

45°

CUT FROM
5/4 x 8
STOCK
(16 REQ'D.)

3" DIA. HOLE

1-1/2" DIA. HOLE

SCREW HOLE

6"

DECORATIVE CORNER BRACE

51-1/2"

22-1/2°

22-1/2°

①

2x4 TOP PLATE
(8 REQ'D.)

4x4 POST
(8 REQ'D.)

90"

79"

④

②

④

3 PER SIDE

9-3/8" x 48" PLASTIC
LATTICE * (15 REQ'D.)

*TRIM TO FIT
AT ASSEMBLY

③

3/4" x 3/4" x 48"
CLEATS * (88 REQ'D.)

HORIZONTAL
TIE

CLEAT

③

WALL
SLAT

SECTION AA

47"

22-1/2°

④

2x4 HORIZONTAL
TIE (33 REQ'D.)

SEE
SECTION AA

34-1/2"

23-1/2"

2"

④

WALL ASSEMBLY

5-1/2" (49 REQ'D.)

2" (14 REQ'D.)

3/4"

19-7/8"

1-1/2"

CUT
FROM
1x6's

WALL SLATS

Fastening Schedule

1. 16d GALV. BOX NAILS
2. 8d GALV. CASING NAILS
3. 4d GALV. FINISH NAILS
4. 3'' GALV. SCREWS

Build the Walls

It's always easiest to work on framing that's laid out on a flat surface rather than upright. So take a tip from the pros and build the walls in sections on the floor, then raise and attach them to each other to complete the frame.

▶ Prebuild four of the seven wall sections (the eighth is the entrance) by attaching horizontal ties between pairs of posts, using 3-inch galvanized deck screws (Photo 7). To speed your work, make a small 22-1/2 degree pie-shaped block to keep each post in position as you screw in each of the ties.

▶ After assembling each section, stand it in position (Photo 8). Brace each section temporarily with a 2x6 screwed to the top of a post to hold the section upright until the gazebo is complete.

▶ With the first sections in place, use the rest of the horizontal wall ties and post cutoffs as spacers to lay out the octagonal shape of the gazebo (Photo 8).

▶ Next, nail the 2x4 top plates to the tops of the posts, then secure 20-gauge metal strap supports to the outsides of the top plates at the corners (see the Construction Plan on page 154 and Photo 9). These metal straps provide a strong supporting band against the outward pressure exerted on the top plates by the weight of the roof.

▶ Lastly, cut and install the corner braces before working on the roof (see the Construction Plan and Photo 10). Use a jigsaw to cut shapes, and 1-1/2 and 3-inch hole saws to make cutouts. Since the vertical edges of the brace pairs have 22-1/2 degree bevels in different directions, make eight left-hand and right-hand pieces (see the Wall Framing Details, opposite).

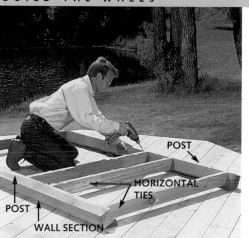

Photo 7. Prebuild four wall sections by screwing horizontal ties to pairs of posts. Run more horizontal ties between these sections to complete the octagon.

Photo 8. Screw each post to the deck with eight 3-in. galvanized deck screws. Use post cutoffs and horizontal ties as spacers.

Photo 9. Nail 20-gauge metal support straps to the outside of each upper corner after nailing the top plates atop the posts, to withstand outward pressure.

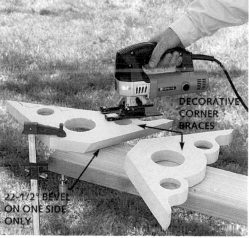

Photo 10. Cut the decorative corner-brace shapes with a jigsaw, using a drill and 1-1/2 and 3-in. hole saws. Make eight left- and eight right-hand pieces.

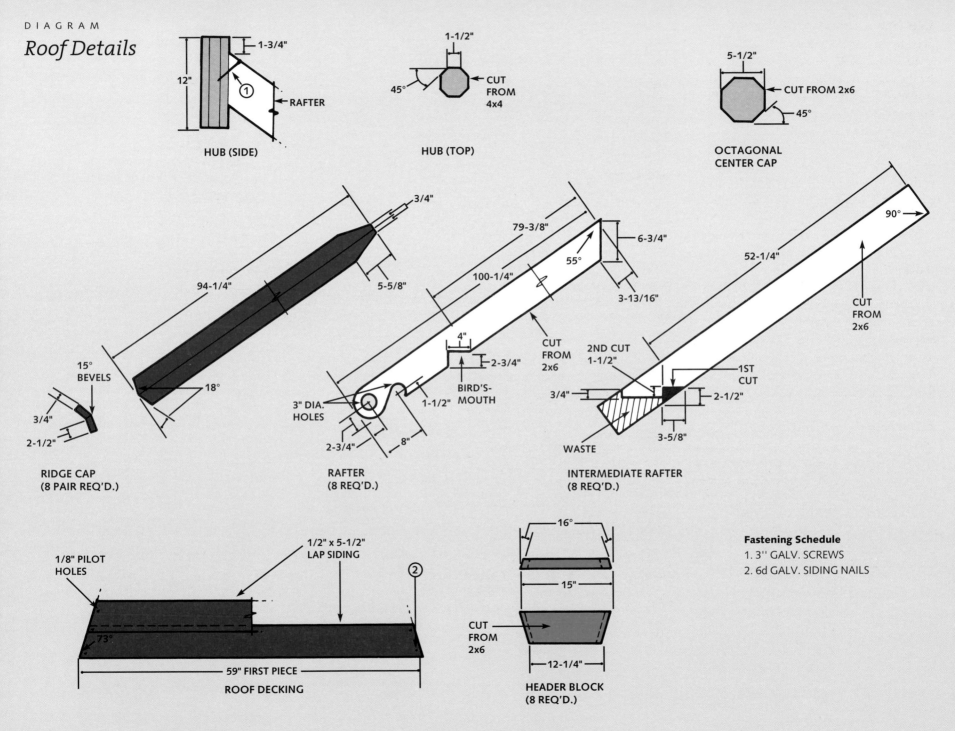

DIAGRAM

Roof Details

1-3/4"

12"

① RAFTER

HUB (SIDE)

1-1/2"

45° CUT FROM 4x4

HUB (TOP)

5-1/2"

CUT FROM 2x6

45°

OCTAGONAL CENTER CAP

3/4"

94-1/4"

5-5/8"

15° BEVELS

3/4"

2-1/2"

18°

RIDGE CAP (8 PAIR REQ'D.)

79-3/8"

55°

6-3/4"

100-1/4"

3-13/16"

4"

2-3/4"

CUT FROM 2x6

BIRD'S-MOUTH

3" DIA. HOLES

1-1/2"

2-3/4"

8"

RAFTER (8 REQ'D.)

52-1/4"

90°

CUT FROM 2x6

2ND CUT 1-1/2"

1ST CUT

3/4"

2-1/2"

WASTE

3-5/8"

INTERMEDIATE RAFTER (8 REQ'D.)

1/8" PILOT HOLES

1/2" x 5-1/2" LAP SIDING

②

73°

59" FIRST PIECE

ROOF DECKING

16°

15"

CUT FROM 2x6

12-1/4"

HEADER BLOCK (8 REQ'D.)

Fastening Schedule
1. 3'' GALV. SCREWS
2. 6d GALV. SIDING NAILS

Cut the Rafters and Slats

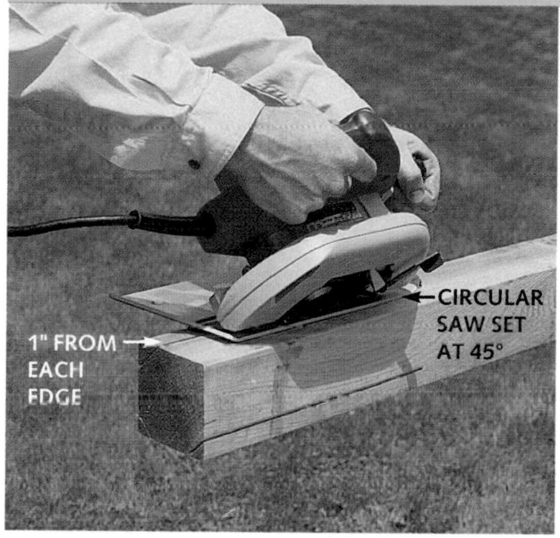

Start by cutting the rafters to the dimensions shown in the Roof Details Diagram on the facing page, but expect to have to trim and shape them a bit for an exact fit. For tips on making compound cuts, see the Techniques box on page 164.

▶ Cut the center hub for the rafters from a 4x4 by beveling the edges at 45 degrees to within 1 inch of each edge (Photo 11). With a handsaw, finish-cut the hub, making it 12 inches long.

▶ Next, cut the rest of the decorative parts: the rafter ends, wall slats, and cleats for the wall slats and the lattice sections. Cut the rafter ends with a jigsaw, after making the holes with a 3-inch hole saw (Photo 12). Then cut the 55-degree angle on the hub end and the notch for the bird's-mouth for the top plate, as in the Roof Details Diagram on the facing page. Finally, round-over any sharp edges with 100-grit sandpaper.

▶ To speed cutting the wall slats, clamp several together and cut the diamond shapes all at once with a circular saw (Photo 13). Set the saw blade at 45 degrees, and cut just deep enough so the kerfs meet at the center.

▶ Cut the cleats for the wall slats and lattice sections a bit long. You can trim them to their exact length later after they have been given a coat of stain.

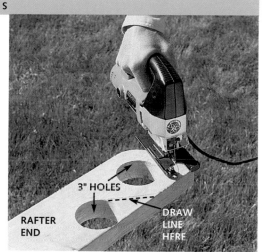

Photo 11. Cut the center hub for the rafters by beveling the edges of a 4x4 at 45 degrees. For safety, make the cuts on a larger piece, then trim to 12 in.

Photo 12. Cut the decorative rafter ends with a jigsaw after cutting the holes shown here with a 3 in. hole saw. Sand down sharp edges with 100-grit paper.

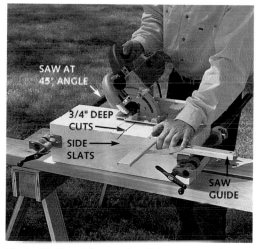

Photo 13. To notch several wall slats at once, clamp them together and cut the diamond shapes with a circular saw. Cut to where the kerfs barely meet.

Making Compound Cuts

Roof framing often calls for making compound cuts to ensure that rafters fit precisely. Compound cuts consist of both a miter cut and a bevel cut. The miter cut is made across the face of the board, the bevel cut through the board's thickness.

To make compound cuts with a circular saw, first set the saw blade for the bevel cut. Next set the protractor-cutting guide at the correct angle for the miter cut. Then, if you follow the protractor guide with your saw table, you'll be able to cut both angles simultaneously.

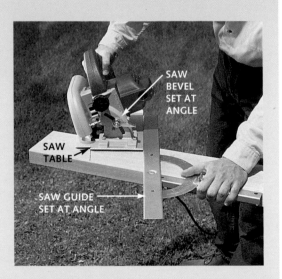

Assemble the Walls and Roof

After the stain is dry, proceed to assemble the walls and roof.

▶ Screw two opposing rafters to the center hub. Then, with a helper, position this "wishbone" across opposite corners of the top plate (Photo 14). Check for fit and recut the bird's-mouth joint if necessary. Toenail each rafter to the 2x4 top plates with 10d galvanized casing nails.

▶ Now, from a ladder positioned inside the gazebo, screw the remaining rafters to the hub, using 3-inch galvanized deck screws. Toenail the rafters to the corners of the top plates with galvanized nails. After the rafters are in position, nail the 2x6 header blocks between them with 10d galvanized casing nails (see the Construction Plan on page 154 and Photo 15).

▶ Next, attach the 2x6 intermediate rafters (see the Construction Plan and Photo 15). Nail them to the headers with 10d galvanized casing nails driven into the ends of the rafters from the top sides of the headers. Then toenail the intermediate rafters to the midpoint of each top plate.

ASSEMBLE THE WALLS AND ROOF

Photo 14. Position the wishbone piece diagonally over opposite posts and onto the top plates. Toenail each rafter to its top plate.

Photo 15. Position the intermediate rafters at the center of each top plate and header block, then nail them in place.

Finish the Job

Before you nail the siding to the rafters, install the wall slats, cleats, and lattice panels, to add structural strength. This gazebo used plastic lattice for lateral support, but wood will also work. Plastic is uniform in thickness and gives the illusion of overlapping strips, is easy to nail, and won't require paint or stain.

Drill pilot holes in the lattice panels and cleats. Use plenty of 4d galvanized finish nails to secure the panels. The gazebo's frame will become more and more solid as you fasten each new panel in place.

Use a carpenter's pencil held sideways to maintain a consistent 1/4-inch space between wall slats. Once the spacing is correct, nail through the cleats into the slats with 4d galvanized finish nails (Photo 16).

▶ To cut the roof siding, start at the bottom of each triangular roof section and work up (Photo 17). Your angled cuts don't have to be precise here, because the ridge caps will cover the joints between sections.

▶ To avoid splitting the siding near edges, drill pilot holes for the galvanized 6d siding nails. To prevent splitting later as the siding expands, locate the nails so they're just above the top of each lower course of siding.

▶ As you work up, nail temporary cleats into the rafters to provide better footing.

▶ When all the siding is in place, nail the octagonal center cap to the top of the hub with 16d galvanized finish nails (Photo 18).

▶ Finally, cut the ridge caps and nail them to the rafters. The ridge caps have a 15-degree bevel on each center edge (see the Roof Details Diagram on page 162). Cut the ridge cap ends to fit neatly around the center cap. Use 8d galvanized casing nails every 8 inches to secure the ridge caps to the rafters.

While you have a ladder at hand, you might want to do a final touch-up on parts you originally stained or painted. Then throw a yard party to enjoy this new addition to your living space.

Finishing Tip

Staining the rafters, wall slats, and cleats before you install them will save a lot of tedious cutting-in with a brush later on.

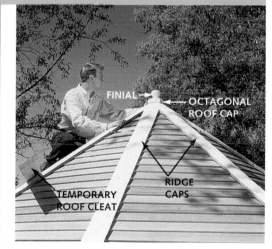

Photo 16. Space the wall slats 1/4 in. apart, using a carpenter's pencil turned sideways as a guide. Nail through the cleats into the slats.

Photo 17. Drill pilot holes and nail the 1-1/2 x 5-1/2 in. cedar lap siding to the rafters with "splitless" 6d galvanized siding nails.

Photo 18. After the ridge caps are in place, nail on the roof cap. Be sure to center it atop the hub. Add the ridge caps and a decorative finial.

Screened Porch

A screened back porch is a great place to relax, breathe some fresh air, and enjoy your

backyard on those warm summer days when you want to get away from the heat

and mosquitoes. With a porch like this you won't have to retreat inside or resort to using

your air conditioner as often. Your porch may just become your favorite summer hangout.

This porch's floor-to-ceiling screens keep it light and airy while holding pesky insects

at bay. The gable is left open to catch stray breezes but is also screened. If the air is quiet,

you can switch on the fan in the cathedral ceiling. And, perhaps best of all,

this porch is large enough to give the kids plenty of play space while leaving

a comfy corner to you.

A screened porch lets you enjoy the best of both worlds: it's a shady, bug-free retreat right in your own backyard, and a permanent, value-enhancing addition to your home.

Construction Plan

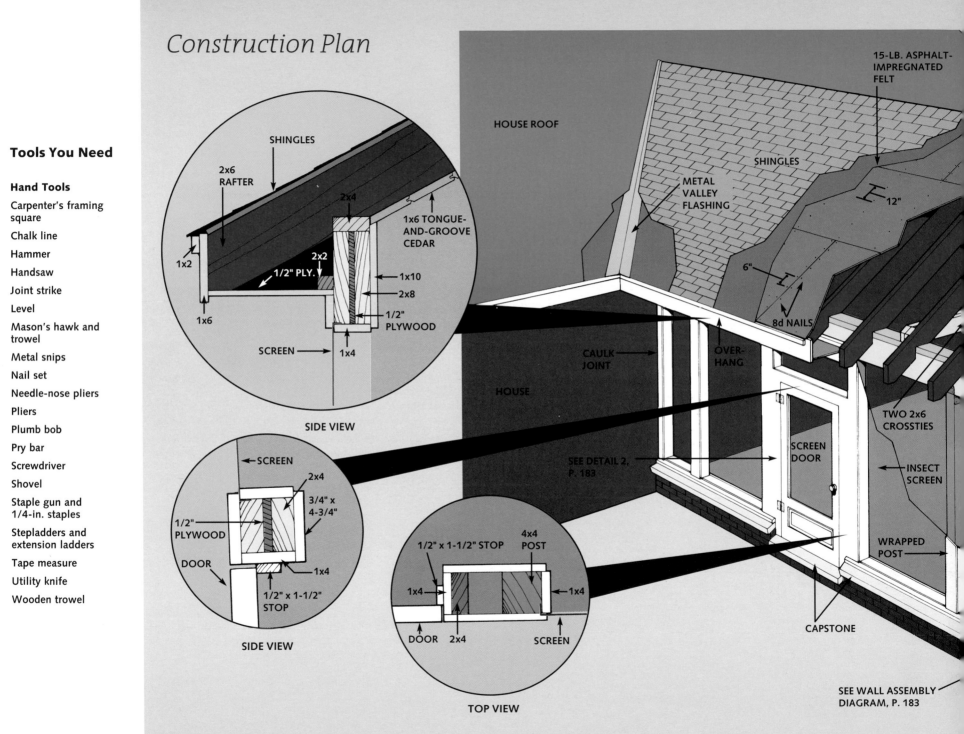

Tools You Need

Hand Tools

Carpenter's framing square

Chalk line

Hammer

Handsaw

Joint strike

Level

Mason's hawk and trowel

Metal snips

Nail set

Needle-nose pliers

Pliers

Plumb bob

Pry bar

Screwdriver

Shovel

Staple gun and 1/4-in. staples

Stepladders and extension ladders

Tape measure

Utility knife

Wooden trowel

SHINGLES

2x6 RAFTER

2x4

1x6 TONGUE-AND-GROOVE CEDAR

1x2

1/2" PLY.

2x2

1x10

2x8

1/2" PLYWOOD

1x6

SCREEN

1x4

SIDE VIEW

HOUSE ROOF

15-LB. ASPHALT-IMPREGNATED FELT

SHINGLES

METAL VALLEY FLASHING

12"

6"

8d NAILS

CAULK JOINT

OVER-HANG

HOUSE

SEE DETAIL 2, P. 183

SCREEN DOOR

TWO 2x6 CROSSTIES

INSECT SCREEN

WRAPPED POST

SCREEN

2x4

3/4" x 4-3/4"

1/2" PLYWOOD

DOOR

1x4

1/2" x 1-1/2" STOP

SIDE VIEW

1/2" x 1-1/2" STOP

4x4 POST

1x4

1x4

DOOR

2x4

SCREEN

TOP VIEW

CAPSTONE

SEE WALL ASSEMBLY DIAGRAM, P. 183

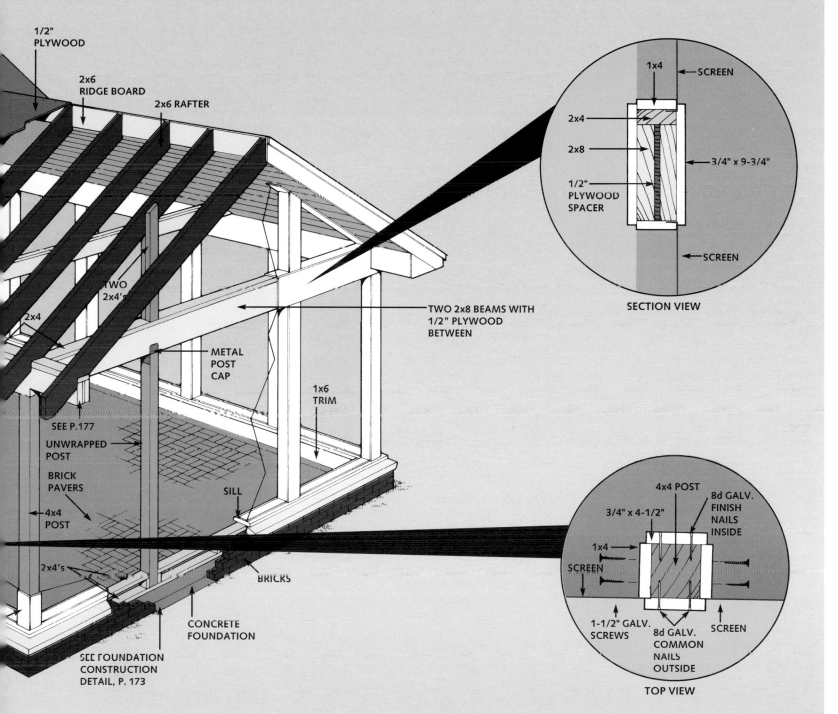

1/2"
PLYWOOD

2x6
RIDGE BOARD

2x6 RAFTER

TWO
2x4's

2x4

TWO 2x8 BEAMS WITH
1/2" PLYWOOD
BETWEEN

METAL
POST
CAP

1x6
TRIM

SEE P.177

UNWRAPPED
POST

BRICK
PAVERS

4x4
POST

SILL

2x4's

BRICKS

CONCRETE
FOUNDATION

SEE FOUNDATION
CONSTRUCTION
DETAIL, P. 173

SECTION VIEW

1x4

SCREEN

2x4

2x8

3/4" x 9-3/4"

1/2"
PLYWOOD
SPACER

SCREEN

TOP VIEW

4x4 POST

8d GALV.
FINISH
NAILS
INSIDE

3/4" x 4-1/2"

1x4

SCREEN

SCREEN

1-1/2" GALV.
SCREWS

8d GALV.
COMMON
NAILS
OUTSIDE

Tools You Need

Power Tools

Circular saw and
masonry blade

Drill

Reciprocating saw

Table saw

Optional Tools

Diamond-blade
masonry saw

Power plate compactor

Power screwdriver

Wheelbarrows

Plan Your Screened Porch

Because this is a warm-weather porch, its screens are designed to be permanent and there are no windows to keep out cold air and rain. In fact, this porch is designed to let any rain that sweeps in drain harmlessly away. However, if you need more weather protection or prefer a three-season porch, you can add permanent windows without changing the basic plans.

Skill and Time Factors

A porch this large and detailed is a formidable project for even the most experienced do-it-yourselfer. Building it yourself will take most of a summer. Don't attempt this project without extensive prior building experience or some professional help.

These instructions will show you the overall step-by-step building techniques, concentrating on the hardest parts: the foundation and the frame. Along the way you'll see a variety of ways to reduce your costs and simplify the design. As with many challenging projects, when you break down this porch design into its many component parts the job becomes less intimidating.

This project often requires at least a second pair of hands. You'll want to recruit a neighbor or friend early on and brief him or her thoroughly on the flow of the project.

Don't hesitate to hire professionals to help with the design, handle difficult parts, or simply speed the project along.

Design Factors

You probably won't want to build this exact porch design. Your home's roof angle may be different, the porch's dimensions may need to be smaller, or the overall style of this porch might require changes to match the appearance of your house. Any one of these factors might necessitate altering the plans shown here.

Whether or not you choose to modify these plans, you'll want your porch to blend seamlessly with your house. When you see a porch that meshes with a house perfectly, you can be assured that someone worked hard to design it that way. To achieve the same results, follow these guidelines.

▶ Design the porch roof to match or complement the main roof of the house. The porch in this project has a gable roof sloped to match the house's gable roof.

▶ Duplicate the trim details that were used on the house. The overhang, or soffit, on this particular porch was designed to match the soffit on the house and was joined to it in such a way as to create continuity in the total appearance.

▶ To blend the porch into your house, use the same building materials. The brick base with its stone cap and the white-painted trim used here accomplish this nicely.

This porch is actually a covered patio. (French doors in the back wall of the house originally opened onto a patio.) Because the first floor of this house is two steps above ground level, the owners located the porch floor one step down from the house. Doing so left the porch floor one step up from the ground, for good drainage. The owners chose brick pavers for the floor, because these are attractive, maintenance-free, and water resistant.

Matching Your House

Because the edges of this porch roof and house roof meet and the soffits of the two structures were designed to match, these homeowners took their porch measurements directly from those for the house. If you do the same thing, use two levels to determine the roof slope, which is the ratio of the vertical rise to the horizontal run. In this case, the ratio was 6 in 12, or a 6-inch rise in 12 inches of roof length.

Once you have the slope, support the roof with doubled 2x8 beams and 4x4 posts, spaced about 4 feet apart. Nail doubled crossties 6 feet apart to keep the walls from bowing outward (see the Construction Plan on the previous two pages).

The foundation itself is concrete, poured to at least 6 inches below the frost depth in the area. Ask your building inspector how deep the frost line runs in your own region. The foundation, which is designed with a special ledge to seat the brick veneering, also serves as a retaining wall for the porch floor, 8 inches above ground level (see the Wall Assembly Diagram on page 183).

For the best appearance of your brick walls and paver floor, plan the foundation's dimensions to fit either whole or half-bricks. If you use standard bricks, make the length of the brick ledge either a multiple of 8 inches (7-5/8 inches for the brick plus 3/8 inch for the mortar joint) or a multiple of 4 inches. Then adjust the wall thickness so the inside dimensions of the floor fit the area of the brick pavers. Paver styles and sizes vary, so lay a dozen of them together on a sheet of plywood and measure them as a test before you plan your final dimensions.

Consulting the Experts

Designing a project this large from scratch takes considerable experience and a knowledge of building principles. Don't hesitate to hire an architect, who will be familiar with area building requirements. And make your local building inspector a partner every step of the way, starting with your initial plans. He or she will make sure your work is soundly conceived and safely carried out so that it is ultimately worth the considerable time and money invested in it.

In any case, prepare a detailed drawing something like the Beams and Rafters detail on page 178, so that your building inspector can examine the project to make sure your foundation, posts, beams, and rafters will be strong enough and the electrical plans meet code requirements. You might prefer to make a separate wiring diagram like the Electrical Circuit Diagram on page 186.

Building Materials List

From your plans, compile a materials list, including everything from the foundation bolts to the screening. This is a key step, because as you account for each piece of lumber on the Construction Plan you'll be able to visualize clearly how everything must fit together. This is also the point at which to identify and solve potential problems before they can contribute to construction delays.

If you choose, you can build your porch even stronger than the one in this design, by making the following modifications.

▶ Use metal post caps, available from any home center or lumberyard, to fasten the 4x4 posts to the 2x4 at the bottom and the doubled 2x8 beam at the top (see the Construction Plan).

▶ Extend the two center posts on the gable end to the rafters instead of stopping at the 2x8 crossbeam (see the Construction Plan). Notch them around the 2x8 beam by cutting through half the beam and half the posts. This will stiffen the walls.

Pour the Foundation

This porch will become part of your house, so it must stand on an equally firm foundation. Sink your concrete footing 12 inches into the ground or at least 6 inches below frost depth (ask the building inspector for this measurement), and make sure it rests on solidly packed soil. To sink the footing without building a complicated form or wooden mold, dig a trench to the proper depth and width, then add a small form to mold the top (see the Foundation Construction Detail on the facing page).

Lay Out the Foundation

▶ First, lay out the dimensions of the trench, using stakes and string lines (Photo 1). Use the house wall as a base line. For a discussion of how to establish right angles, see "Mark Your Layout" on page 25. Check the diagonal measurements; when they're equal, your foundation is perfectly square.

▶ Check with your gas, water, and electric utility companies before you dig, to avoid disturbing any underground services.

Dig the Trench

▶ Dig the trench now. You will no doubt discover this to be hard work. Two people can complete the job in about one day. It may take considerably longer, however, if sizable rocks are in the way. Keep a heavy steel pry bar handy for this purpose. Look for one that is 5 feet long and weighs more than 20 pounds.

▶ Angle the sides of the trench outward as you go down, so that the bottom of the trench is wider than the top, to prevent frost heaves. Flatten the bottom to match the profile in the Foundation Construction Detail at right and Photo 2. If the soil is too soft and caves in, line the trench sides with rigid foam insulation or scraps of plywood.

LAY OUT THE FOUNDATION

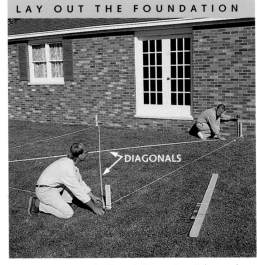

Photo 1. Lay out the foundation, using stakes and a string line. Measure the diagonals to make sure they're of equal length.

DIG THE TRENCH

Photo 2. Dig a trench 10 in. wide and at least 12 in. deep, or at least 6 in. below the frost line. Flare the bottom of the trench to 15 in. wide.

Foundation Construction

Make sure that the foundation you pour rests firmly on flat, undisturbed soil 12 in. down—or at least 6 in. below the frost line. Check the depth needed for footings in your area—you may have to go deeper.

Broaden the base, as shown here, so that normal freeze-thaw cycles will not thrust the foundation upward. Level the 4-in. brick ledge by forming it with 2x4's or larger stock. For tips on foundation framing, see page 174.

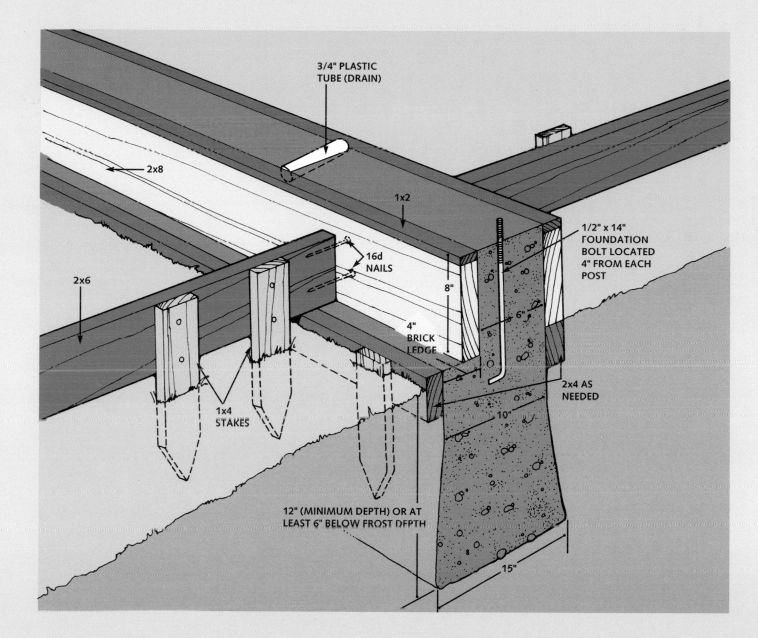

3/4" PLASTIC TUBE (DRAIN)

2x8

1x2

1/2" x 14" FOUNDATION BOLT LOCATED 4" FROM EACH POST

16d NAILS

8"

2x6

4" BRICK LEDGE

6"

2x4 AS NEEDED

1x4 STAKES

10"

12" (MINIMUM DEPTH) OR AT LEAST 6" BELOW FROST DEPTH

15"

Frame the Trench

▶ Frame the top of the trench with 2x8's, because the new concrete foundation will extend 8 inches above the ground (Photo 3). These 2x8's will measure only 7-1/4 inches wide, so nail 1x2 strips to their tops to add the extra 3/4 inch you'll need. You should be able to clean and reuse most of the 2x8's for your porch beams.

▶ Build the outer form first, cutting the sides as shown in the Construction Plan on pages 168–169. Position the form with string lines, then level it and stake it in place. The form actually hangs suspended over the trench as in Photo 3. It is anchored by 1x4 stakes and 2x6's that resist the pressure of the concrete filling the form. Make sure your form is strong—it must be rock solid when you pour the concrete.

▶ Once the outer form is completed, cut and set the inner form in the same way.

Few backyards are perfectly flat. The yard shown here sloped away from the house, leaving the brick ledge exposed above-ground on the low side of the porch. Keep the 4-inch brick ledge level as necessary by forming the ledge with 2x4's or larger stock, depending upon the slope.

▶ Allow plenty of time to level the forms and position them accurately before ready-mixed concrete is delivered. Working under pressure can result in mistakes that will be difficult to correct after the concrete hardens. With a tape, measure the diagonals of the form to make sure they're equal and that the form is perfectly square. Then sight down the length of each form section to make sure it's straight. Use a crayon to mark the exact positions of the posts and the doorway. Mark a point about 4 inches from each post for a foundation bolt, and locate 3/4-inch plastic drain tubes every 4 feet. Have all bolts and drains ready to place in the wet concrete.

▶ Now, ask your building inspector to check your work before you proceed.

▶ Calculate the volume of concrete you'll need, and order it ready-mixed. To determine the number of cubic yards needed, multiply the number of feet of width of the foundation times its depth (in other words, the area of the cross-section in the Foundation Construction Detail on page 173) times its length. The arithmetic can become a bit complicated because of the slanted sides of the trench, so it's best to overestimate by a few cubic feet to be sure of having enough.

▶ Because the construction site for your back porch will of course be behind your home, the delivery truck may not be able to get close enough to pour directly into your forms. Check whether the truck might have an extension chute capable of reaching the forms you've built, or whether it is equipped with a pump to deliver the concrete through a hose. If not, the solution is to recruit several helpers, rent three or four strong wheelbarrows, and be prepared to work quickly once the concrete arrives.

▶ As you fill the forms, thrust a shovel or a 1x2 into the fresh concrete to help it settle against the trench sides and into the corners.

▶ Finally, use a wooden trowel to flatten the top and level the brick ledge (Photo 4). Then push the foundation bolts and drains into place in the locations you marked (Photo 5). Cover the concrete with plastic and let it cure for several days before you pull off the forms.

▶ Once you have removed the forms, you can begin the actual building of the porch.

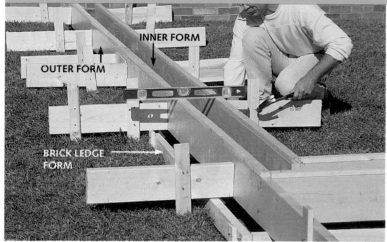

INNER FORM

OUTER FORM

BRICK LEDGE FORM

Photo 3. Brace and stake the forms so they're straight and level. Form the ledge for the low brick wall where the form is aboveground.

Photo 4. Fill the trench and forms with ready-mixed concrete. Smooth the top and the brick ledge with a wooden trowel.

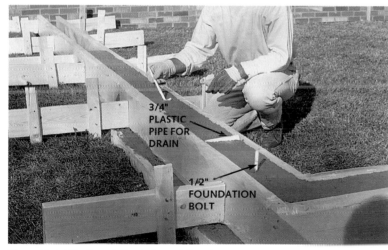

3/4" PLASTIC PIPE FOR DRAIN

1/2" FOUNDATION BOLT

Photo 5. Set the foundation bolts and the 3/4-in. plastic drains into the concrete. Space the plastic drains about every 4 ft.

Frame the Walls

Prepare the Sills and Rafters

▶ Break off the exposed parts of the plastic drains, then lay a special sill seal to keep the wood dry (Photo 6). Cut pressure-treated 2x4's for the sill plates, drill them to accept the foundation bolts, and cinch them down.

▶ Now cut into the house. With a level or a plumb bob, find a vertical line up the side of the house from the sill plate to the roof overhang (Photo 7). Cut the overhang at this point, then remove the unwanted section over the porch. You should now be able to see the rafters and doubled top plate of your house, as shown in the Corner and Wall Connections Details on the facing page.

▶ Next, cut back the roof overhang. Use a worn saw blade to cut through the roofing; the shingles will dull a new blade. Trim the rafters back, saving the cutoff pieces to use as nailers for the interior paneling.

▶ Finally, cut and remove a 3-1/2 inch notch out of the top 2x4 on the house's doubled top plate where the walls attach (see the details on the opposite page). This gap provides space for the 2x4's that will be nailed to the top of the beam to lap over and fasten the porch walls to the house (Photo 8). Perform this step carefully to avoid damaging interior walls.

Assemble the Porch Beams

Now cut and assemble the porch beams, making them long enough to butt against the house's sheathing or framing. Note that the beams should be longer than the foundation, because they extend out over the brick.

▶ Nail a 2x4 on top of the beams to tie the corners together (see the Corner and Wall Connections Details at right).

▶ Now cut the 4x4 posts to length, using a circular saw and a handsaw to finish the cuts if necessary.

▶ Mark the rafter locations on the tops of the beams before assembling the walls. It's much easier to do this while the beams are still on the ground.

PREPARE THE SILLS AND RAFTERS

Photo 6. Lay a sill seal on the foundation, bolt the bottom plates down, and nail the 4x4 posts to the plates with four 16d nails. Brace the posts with boards.

Photo 7. Cut back the shingles and roof sheathing, remove the part of the trim and soffit that overhangs the porch, and trim back the rafter ends.

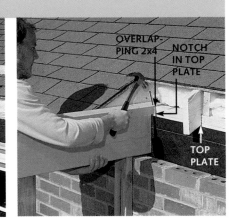

Photo 8. Set the top 2x4 into a notch cut into the top plate of the house wall. Secure it with four 16d galvanized nails.

Corner and Wall Connections

As you prepare to frame the new porch's walls and roof and connect them to the house, refer to these details and see how they fit in to the overall Construction Plan on pages 168–169. The outer, freestanding corners are constructed according to the top diagram at right. The two inner walls attach to the house as shown.

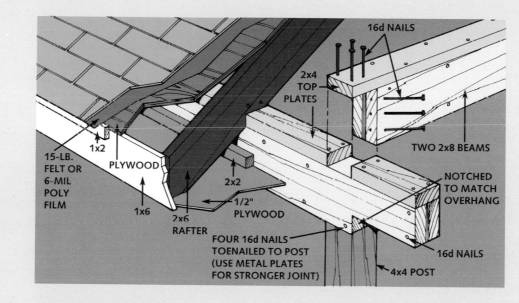

CONNECTING THE CORNERS

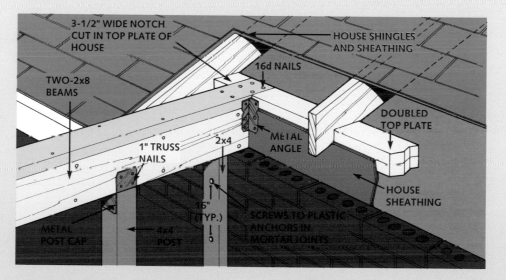

CONNECTING THE WALLS TO THE HOUSE

Erect the Walls

▶ To erect the walls, first nail each 4x4 to its sill with four 16d galvanized nails. Then screw the two 2x4 plates to the brick wall of the house (see the Corner and Wall Connections Details on page 177).

▶ Next, brace each 4x4 corner securely with two 1x6 boards. These braces are absolutely critical, to ensure the posts' stability when setting the heavy beams on them. It will take at least two people to walk the beams up ladders and set them on the posts (Photo 9).

▶ Nail the 2x4 top plates at the corners to fasten the beams together. Then toenail the beams to the posts, the house, and each other at the corners. Toenail at a 45-degree angle starting about one-third of a nail length up the board. For stronger connections, use metal post caps and angles (see the details on page 177).

▶ Finally, use a carpenter's level to make sure all the posts are standing perfectly vertical along one side. Temporarily brace them as necessary. Then toenail the two crossties in place, making sure the other wall is perfectly vertical as well (Photo 10).

Photo 9. Assemble the beams and, with at least one other helper, set them on top of the posts. Attach the corners together with 16d galvanized nails.

Photo 10. Toenail the crossties in place with four 16d galvanized nails. Brace the walls to make sure they stand perfectly vertical.

DETAIL
Beams and Rafters

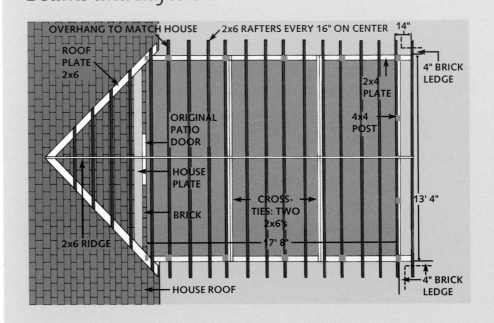

Frame the Roof

Lay Out and Cut the Rafters

Except for the short rafters that sit on the roof of the house, the rafters on the porch roof are identical. Once you determine the size of one rafter, use it as a template to mark all the others.

The traditional method of determining rafter length uses a framing square (follow the sequence in the diagram for laying out a rafter on the next page), but you can also use geometry and a calculator. Do use a framing square to find the angles of the ridge, seat, and tail cuts. If this is your first attempt at building a roof and you are unsure about it, refer to a book on basic framing or hire a carpenter.

After cutting the first two rafters, test-fit them on the walls to make sure their angles are correct. Insert a 1-1/2 inch board between them to represent the ridge board.

If the rafters don't fit properly, stop and rework the entire pattern until you find the error. Then, using one rafter as a pattern, cut the rest, making sure any warp in the rafters bows upward. (The roof's weight will help straighten any warped rafters.)

▶ Next, mark the rafter locations every 16 inches on center on a 2x6 ridge board (see the Beams and Rafters Detail on the facing page). The ridge of this particular porch is about 25 feet long and required two 2x6's, joined at the center where two rafters meet.

▶ To assemble the rafters, nail opposite pairs to the ridge board and to the top plates of the walls. Begin by nailing one end of the outer ridge board to a temporary brace (the height doesn't have to be exact). Then nail a pair of rafters near the other end (Photo 11). Toenail the seat of one rafter to the top plate with three 16d galvanized nails, then drive another three 16d nails through the ridge board into the top end of the rafter. Repeat this process with the opposite rafter (Photo 12).

▶ Nail a temporary second brace at an angle from a crosstie to the ridge board near the first rafters to stabilize the ridge board.

▶ Release the first brace. Nail a second pair of rafters three rafter spaces (3 x 16 inches, or 48 inches) in from the outer end of the ridge board, to level it so you can fill in the other rafters, a pair at a time. Install the two pairs of outermost rafters last.

▶ With a straight board and a level make sure the rafters over the end wall are perfectly aligned with the wall. Rebrace as necessary.

For this roof, the crossties are set so that a pair of rafters lies along them (see the detail, opposite). For stability, nail rafters to crossties with three 16d nails.

LAY OUT AND CUT THE RAFTERS

RIDGE BOARD

BRACE

RAFTER

Photo 11. Nail a rafter to the ridge board and the top plate of the porch with three 16d nails at each end. Brace the other end of the ridge board temporarily.

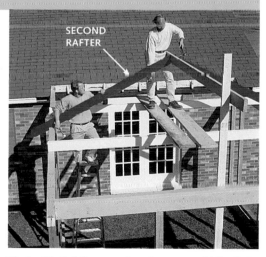

SECOND RAFTER

Photo 12. Nail the opposite rafter as you did the first. Then nail a pair of rafters near the braced end of the ridge board and add the others in between.

Laying Out a Rafter

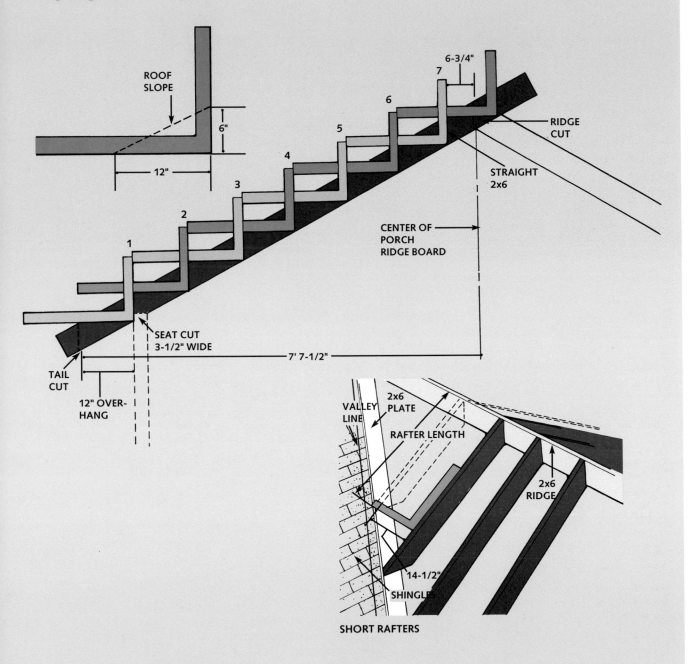

ROOF SLOPE

6"

12"

6-3/4"

7

6

5

4

3

2

1

RIDGE CUT

STRAIGHT 2x6

CENTER OF PORCH RIDGE BOARD

SEAT CUT 3-1/2" WIDE

TAIL CUT

12" OVER-HANG

7' 7-1/2"

VALLEY LINE

2x6 PLATE

RAFTER LENGTH

2x6 RIDGE

14-1/2"

SHINGLES

SHORT RAFTERS

Install Ridge Boards

After all the rafters have been connected to the outer ridge board, proceed to install the inner ridge board.

▶ First, determine where this inner ridge board will meet the roof. One way to locate this point is simply to extend the ridge-board-to-be over to the roof (Photo 13). With the board level, mark the roof in several locations and connect those points to establish a level line (represented by the 2x4 across the roof in Photo 13). Now find the center line, the point on the level line that is an equal distance from each corner where the porch adjoins the house.

▶ Cut the ridge board to length, then cut the roof slope on the other end. Nail it to the roof and to the rafters where it meets the first ridge board.

INSTALL RIDGE BOARDS

RIDGE HEIGHT

RIDGE LENGTH

CENTER LINE

Photo 13. Position the inner ridge board, extend it over to the roof, and level it to confirm that it's positioned correctly. Then cut it to length.

Install Short Rafters

▶ Continue to install pairs of rafters until you reach the roof of the house (see the Beams and Rafters Detail on page 178). Now nail 2x6 plates to the roof and cut the shorter rafters. To position the 2x6's, first snap chalk lines on the shingles from the tip of the ridge to the two points where the porch roof meets the lower edge of the house roof (again, see the Beams and Rafters Detail).

▶ Cut 2x6's as shown in the detail and fasten them to the roof about an inch below the chalk lines with 16d galvanized nails driven through the shingles and into the house rafters below (Photo 14). (If you have three or more layers of shingles on your roof, you'll have to remove at least one layer in this area so that the nails can penetrate the rafters.) The bottom face of the roof sheathing that you will add later should fall on the chalk lines.

▶ Determine the length of the short rafters by laying a framing square along the last rafter and measuring 14-1/2 inches to the next one. Mark the edge of the 2x6 roof plate where the short rafter will sit (see the detail on page 178).

▶ Measure the length of the first pair of short rafters, cut and install them, and repeat the process for the next pair. Make the ridge and seat cuts at the same angle as for the other rafters, but tilt your saw blade to match the angle of the roof slope for the seat cuts (Photo 15).

▶ Attach the 1/2-inch plywood roof sheathing with 8d galvanized nails when all the rafters are in place. Space the nails 6 inches apart at the edges of the roof and 12 inches apart in the middle. Also nail the sheathing to the 2x6 roof plates that you attached to the house roof. This connection helps stabilize the entire porch roof. Then install the trim boards along the roof edges with 8d galvanized nails to prepare for the shingles (Photo 16).

INSTALL SHORT RAFTERS

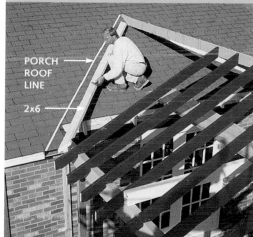

Photo 14. Fasten two 2x6 roof plates along the lines where the porch roof meets the house roof, using 16d galvanized nails.

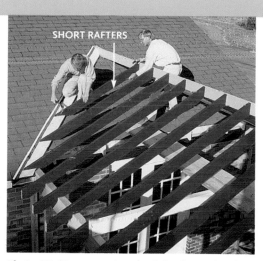

Photo 15. Measure, cut, and nail the short rafters in place. Then install the 1/2-in. plywood roof sheathing using 8d galvanized nails.

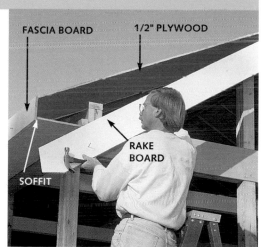

Photo 16. Install the trim boards along the edges of the roof, using 8d galvanized nails. To blend the porch with the house, try to duplicate the house trim.

Working on a Roof

Sweep the roof lightly before you start, to remove tree debris or anything else you could slip on.

For a secure foothold while working on your roof, rent a pair of roof jacks from your roofing materials supplier. Slip each jack under a shingle in your work area, then nail them in place. To make a scaffold, place a 2x6 across the jacks for your foothold. Once you're done, slide the jacks out and hammer the nails in flush with the surface of the roof.

On a steep roof, anchor a ladder in place with ladder braces, which hook over the peak of the roof. You can buy these at a building-supply store.

To keep your hand tools from sliding off the roof, lay down sheets of the soft plastic foam used as cushioning in packages. They'll grip the roof and hold your tools to prevent them from skidding away from you and possibly falling on someone below. Keep bystanders safely away from the house anyway, just to be safe.

Avoid power lines—they are not always insulated.

Leakproof the Joints

The porch-to-house roof joint is the one most susceptible to leaks. Follow these steps to keep it watertight.

▶ With a utility knife, cut through the old shingles 2 inches beyond the valley where the porch sheathing meets the house roof.

▶ Bend the shingles back along this valley, prying up any roofing nails that fall within 8 inches of the cut.

▶ Slide 15-pound roofing felt and special galvanized valley flashing under the shingles (Photo 17). Tack the shingles back down— but only along the outer edge of the valley flashing, not toward its middle.

Add more felt and flashing. Overlap the layers below by 4 inches.

▶ Now add gutters if they are part of your design, then nail on the shingles. You will find complete instructions on each package of shingles.

▶ Finally, ask your building inspector if there are additional steps you may need to take to have the roof meet your local building code.

▶ After completing and roofing the porch structure, move on to the wall details and finish work called for in your design.

LEAKPROOF THE JOINTS

VALLEY FLASHING

15-LB. FELT OR 6-MIL. FILM

Photo 17. Cut the house shingles, then tuck 15-lb. roofing felt or 6-mil polyethylene film and galvanized valley flashing 8 in. underneath adjacent shingles.

Wall Assembly

The plan at right indicates how the wall in this project was constructed out of pressure-treated 2x4's covered outside with treated 1/2-inch plywood. Detail 1 is a section showing how the wall was built up out of 4 bricks plus a capstone and a cedar trim sill. The final finish is shown in Detail 2.

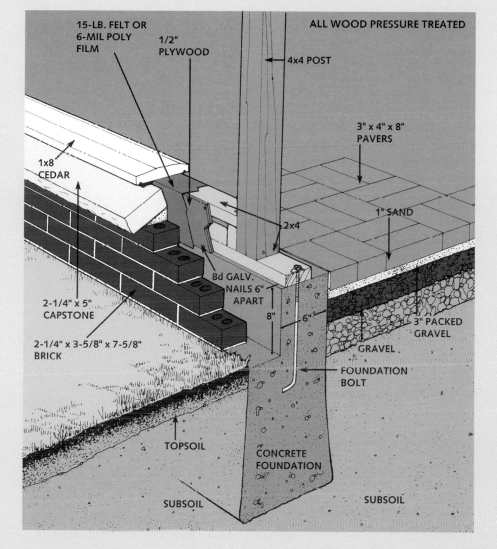

- 15-LB. FELT OR 6-MIL POLY FILM
- 1/2" PLYWOOD
- ALL WOOD PRESSURE TREATED
- 4x4 POST
- 1x8 CEDAR
- 3" x 4" x 8" PAVERS
- 1" SAND
- 2x4
- 8d GALV. NAILS 6" APART
- 2-1/4" x 5" CAPSTONE
- 2-1/4" x 3-5/8" x 7-5/8" BRICK
- 8"
- 6"
- 3" PACKED GRAVEL
- GRAVEL
- FOUNDATION BOLT
- TOPSOIL
- CONCRETE FOUNDATION
- SUBSOIL
- SUBSOIL

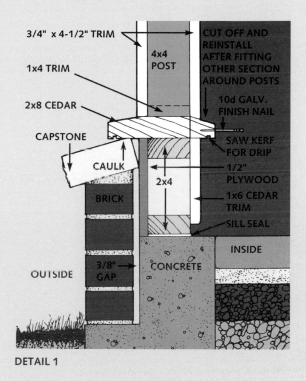

- 3/4" x 4-1/2" TRIM
- 4x4 POST
- CUT OFF AND REINSTALL AFTER FITTING OTHER SECTION AROUND POSTS
- 1x4 TRIM
- 10d GALV. FINISH NAIL
- 2x8 CEDAR
- SAW KERF FOR DRIP
- CAPSTONE
- 1/2" PLYWOOD
- CAULK
- 2x4
- BRICK
- 1x6 CEDAR TRIM
- SILL SEAL
- INSIDE
- OUTSIDE
- 3/8" GAP
- CONCRETE

DETAIL 1

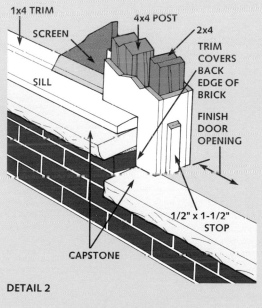

- 1x4 TRIM
- SCREEN
- 4x4 POST
- 2x4
- SILL
- TRIM COVERS BACK EDGE OF BRICK
- FINISH DOOR OPENING
- 1/2" x 1-1/2" STOP
- CAPSTONE

DETAIL 2

Complete the Walls

Finish the Structure

These homeowners bridged the spaces between posts with low walls, using pressure-treated 2x4's, and covered them on the outside with 1/2-inch pressure-treated plywood (see the details on the last page and Photo 18 below).

▶ Attach the plywood with 8d galvanized nails spaced every 6 inches, driving at least four nails into every post to anchor the posts to the foundation. These homeowners designed the height of the low wall to equal the four rows of brick plus the special capstone indicated in Detail 1 on page 183.

▶ Frame the screen door with pressure-treated 2x4's (see the Side and Top views on page 168 and Detail 2 on the previous page).

▶ After covering the plywood with 15-pound felt to protect the wall from dampness, shape and notch 2x8 cedar sections to fit around the posts and form a finished sill (see Photo 19 and Detail 1, page 183). Nail the cedar wrapping in place with 10d galvanized finish nails.

Lay the Brick Support Wall

Even if you're not an experienced bricklayer, if you take your time and work carefully you can build this handsome low brick wall.

The key to good bricklaying is to keep the rows perfectly straight and vertical. If your concrete foundation is straight and level, that will help guide your work. Space 3-5/8 inch bricks 3/8 inch away from the foundation and snap chalk lines on the foundation to guide the height of each row. Or do as the pros do and stretch a cord tightly at the height of each row, then work along that guide. Use a level to ensure that you lay each brick perfectly flat.

FINISH THE STRUCTURE

1/2" TREATED PLYWOOD

Photo 18. Build the short walls with pressure-treated 2x4's. Cover them with 1/2-in. pressure-treated plywood attached with 8d galvanized nails.

NOTCHED SILL

INSIDE SILL PIECE

15-LB. FELT OR 6-MIL POLY FILM

Photo 19. Form 2x8 cedar sills with a table saw, notch them to fit around the posts, and secure them in place with 10d galvanized finish nails.

Build the Brick Wall

To build the brick wall, follow these steps.

▶ Count the number of bricks you'll need, add 5 percent for damage and spares, and have the dealer deliver them as close to the job site as possible. Also have the dealer help you estimate the amount of mortar you'll need and deliver it, too.

▶ Beginning at the outer corners, stretch a measuring tape on the foundation and mark the positions of the bricks in the first row. By narrowing or widening the joints between the bricks, you can make your brick pattern fit each side, using only whole or half-bricks. Also plan the pattern around the doorway.

▶ Mix about 20 pounds of mortar to a consistency that will let it stick to your trowel, then lay the first row of bricks. If the mortar begins to stiffen, add a little water and remix it. Mix no more mortar than you'll be able to use in about an hour.

▶ Lay a bed of mortar about 3/4 inch thick, "butter" one brick end with mortar, and set it in place (Photo 20). Tap the brick down into its exact position with the butt end of your trowel. Mortar should squeeze out of the joints. Leave all the end joints open below the plastic drains, to let water escape.

▶ Lay the first row, then build up the corners, using your level to keep the bricks perfectly vertical and flat. Now fill in the rest of the wall.

▶ About five minutes after laying a section, run a special striking tool over the joints to knock off excess mortar, compact the joint, and shape it to match the pointing of the joints on your house.

▶ Unless you're experienced in the brick-cracking technique that professional bricklayers use, cut your bricks with a special masonry blade in a circular saw. Bricks are usually soft and fairly easy to cut.

▶ You can also saw the capstones with a masonry blade, or rent a special saw with a diamond blade. Dampen the capstones before setting them, so the mortar will stick to them. When you position the capstones, give them a slight outward tilt so that rainwater will run off (see Detail 1 on page 183 and Photo 21). The 2x8 cedar trim sill shown in Photo 19 is installed with the other trim at the end of the job.

Matching Brick

Manufacturers change brick colors often, so you might have a problem finding the right size and color of bricks to match your home. But even if the match isn't perfect, the contrast will show only where new bricks meet old. Position a shrub to hide this joint.

BUILD THE BRICK WALL

"BUTTERING" THE BRICK

LEVEL LINES

JOINT TOOL

MORTAR BED

Photo 20. Snap chalk lines on the foundation for a guide, then lay the first row of bricks along them. Use a level to keep the wall flat and perfectly vertical.

CAPSTONE TILTED FOR WATER RUNOFF

Photo 21. Trim the capstones with a masonry blade in a circular saw, moisten their undersides, and lay them at an angle in a bed of mortar.

Add the Finishing Touches

Lay the Pavers

Brick pavers, which are baked harder than standard bricks, make an attractive floor all by themselves, as do many other combinations of concrete, stone, and pavers. You can make your new porch floor decorative or keep it simple and cover it with something like woven mats. In any case, expect it to get wet. Because rain will blow in, lay the center of the floor so it's about an inch higher than the edges for proper drainage. Or simply slant the entire floor slightly in one direction, about 1 inch in 8 feet.

You can install the pavers anytime after you have prepared the foundation (Photo 22). For complete information on laying brick pavers, see "Patio and Pathway" (pages 92–103).

Run Electrical Lines

To enjoy this porch most thoroughly, you'll want to be able to use it at night. The low support walls were therefore designed to provide enough space to run wires and install receptacles.

Install the Wiring

Place the receptacles within 6 feet of a door and 12 feet of each other, measured along the wall (see the Electrical Circuit Diagram, below). In this case, holes were drilled right into the porch wall from the basement.

Run your wires through holes drilled exactly into the centers of the posts so that nails won't interfere with them. If your house is built on a concrete slab, you might need to run the wiring down the house wall from the attic or bring it in from below, perhaps through the concrete foundation. In any case, plan the wiring in advance and get

LAY THE PAVERS

CONCRETE EDGES

SAND BED

PAVERS

Photo 22. Lay the brick pavers on a tightly packed bed of special gravel topped with a level, 1-in. bed of coarse washed sand.

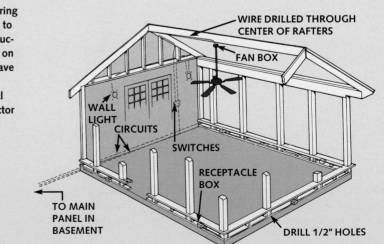

DIAGRAM

Electrical Circuit

If you sketch your wiring in a diagram like this to go along with the structural diagram shown on page 178, you will have a full set of plans to discuss with the local building-code inspector to gain approval to proceed.

WIRE DRILLED THROUGH CENTER OF RAFTERS

FAN BOX

WALL LIGHT

CIRCUITS

SWITCHES

RECEPTACLE BOX

TO MAIN PANEL IN BASEMENT

DRILL 1/2" HOLES

your plans approved by your local electrical inspector before proceeding.

The detail here shows one way to run the circuits. In this example a wire from the main panel enters the switch box, which operates the overhead fan and the lights.

Protecting Against Shock

Because of the potential shock hazard of operating a switch while standing on a damp floor, install either ground fault circuit interrupter (GFCI) receptacles or connect standard receptacles to a ground fault interrupter circuit breaker at the main service panel. Because the receptacles themselves will be exposed to the elements, you must also install special waterproof covers on their boxes (Photo 23). For more about electrical protection, see page 77.

Trim Posts and Ceiling Rafters

To dress up this porch and help it blend with the trim of the house, these homeowners wrapped the posts and beams with pine sections, then painted them. The trim pieces were cut to size with a bench saw. However, you may decide to use simpler trim or choose to leave the sections exposed.

To duplicate the trim used here, first nail tongue-and-groove 1x6 cedar strips to the undersides of the rafters. If you plan to enclose your porch later, insulate the rafter spaces now and install a vapor barrier, shiny side down, before nailing up the paneling.

See the Construction Plan on pages 168–169 for details on the sizes and placement of the rafter and wall-base trim pieces. If you choose to use less-expensive knotty pine instead of a better grade of wood, be sure to coat the knots with a special sealer so

they won't bleed through the paint's top coat. Then nail the trim boards in place with 8d galvanized nails.

Attach Insect Screening

As you install the outer trim pieces, attach fiberglass insect screening to the back sides of the trim pieces or posts, whichever works best. Use 1/4-inch staples (Photo 24). This is a two-person job requiring one to draw the screening tight while the other staples it in place. Screw the last pieces of trim in place so that you can remove them later to repair the screens (Photo 25).

Complete the Job

Finally, hang a new wooden screen door in the doorway opening. Then give the trim pieces one last coat of paint and pull up a new porch swing to watch it dry.

RUN ELECTRICAL LINES

RECEPTACLE CONNECTED TO GFCI AT MAIN PANEL

WEATHERPROOF COVER

Photo 23. Pull in wiring from the house, run it through 1/2-in. holes drilled through the centers of the posts, and mount receptacle boxes and lights.

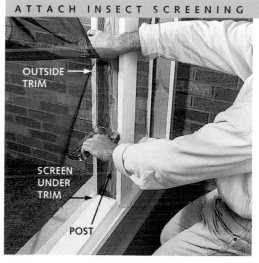

ATTACH INSECT SCREENING

OUTSIDE TRIM

SCREEN UNDER TRIM

POST

Photo 24. Staple screening first to the back sides of the outer trim pieces or posts and then to the finished sill. Use 1/4-in. staples.

Photo 25. Screw in the last trim pieces that cover the staples. You'll need to be able to remove them later to repair the screens.

Index

Acknowledgments

Jim Adami, Ron Chamberlain, John Emmons, Bill Faber, Bruce Folke, Al Hildenbrand, Duane Johnson, Bruce Kieffer, Mike Krivit, Rich Laffin, Travis Larson, Phil Leisenheimer, Don Mannes, Susan Moore, Dale Mulfinger, Doug Oudekerk, Don Prestly, Tim Quigley, Dave Radtke, Art Rooze, Paul Rusten, Julia Schreifels, Rich Sill, Mike Smith, Dan Stoffel, Eugene Thompson, Mark Thompson, Bob Ungar, Alice Wagner, Gregg Weigand, Gary Wentz, Michaela Wentz, Gordy Wilkinson, John Williamson, Marcia Williston, Donna Wyttenbach, Bill Zuehlke.

This book was produced by Roundtable Press, Inc., for the Reader's Digest Association in cooperation with The Family Handyman magazine. If you have any questions or comments, please feel free to write us at:

The Family Handyman
7900 International Drive
Suite 950
Minneapolis, MN 55425

Measuring the Metric Way

Use these guides and table to convert between English and metric measuring systems.

Fasteners

Nails are sold by penny size or penny weight (expressed by the letter *d*). Length is designated by the penny size. Some common lengths are:

2d	25 mm/1 in.
6d	51 mm/2 in.
10d	76 mm/3 in.
20d	102 mm/4 in.
40d	127 mm/5 in.
60d	152 mm/6 in.

Below are approximate metric and imperial equivalents of some common **bolts**:

10 mm	⅜ in.
12 mm	½ in.
16 mm	⅝ in.
20 mm	¾ in.
25 mm	1 in.
50 mm	2 in.
65 mm	2½ in.
70 mm	2¾ in.

Calculating Concrete Requirements

Multiply length by width to get the slab area in square meters. Then read across, under whichever of three thicknesses you prefer, to see how many cubic meters of concrete you will need.

Area in Square Meters (m²)	Thickness in Millimeters		
(length x width)	100	130	150
	Volume in Cubic Meters (m³)		
5	0.50	0.65	0.75
10	1.00	1.30	1.50
20	2.00	2.60	3.00
30	3.00	3.90	4.50
40	4.00	5.20	6.00
50	5.00	6.50	7.50

If a greater volume of concrete is required, multiply by the appropriate number. To lay a 100-millimeter thick patio in an area 6 meters wide and 10 meters long, for example, estimate as follows: 6 meters x 10 meters = 60 meters square = area. Using the chart above, simply double the concrete quantity for a 30-meter square, 100-millimeter thick slab (2 x 3 m³ = 6 m³) or add the quantities for 10 m² and 50 m² (1 m³ + 5 m³ = 6 m³).